THE SEVEN WONDERS OF HIS STORY

THE SEVEN WONDERS
OF HIS STORY

David Pawson

Anchor Recordings

First published in 2012
by Anchor Recordings Ltd
72 The Street, Kennington, Ashford TN24 9HS UK

www.davidpawson.com
For further information, email info@davidpawsonministry.com

www.davidpawson.org

ISBN 978-0-9569376-5-0

Printed in Great Britain by
Imprint Digital, Exeter
Printed in USA by CreateSpace.com

Contents

Prologue

WHOSE STORY?

Reg was the chief accountant for the British Overseas Airways Corporation (B.O.A.C.), forerunner to British Airways (BA). He was also a Scoutmaster in his spare time. He lived in Buckinghamshire with his family. He had three sons, one of whom was later tragically swept overboard when the fated Fastnet yacht race hit an unexpected Atlantic storm. All five of them regularly attended our church in Chalfont St. Peter. Most would have thought he was a 'good' Christian, but they would have been wrong.

He never sang any of the hymns with us but stood silently with shut mouth. When I asked him about this he told me he wouldn't be dishonest and sing what he didn't believe and couldn't mean. I was profoundly challenged by his honesty and my respect for him grew. Ever since then I have refrained from singing anything that was not real for me, a reticence that has increased with the deluge of new songs used in worship, often more sentimental than scriptural.

Then one Sunday, not long after I had become the pastor, I noticed that he was singing, with his whole heart and soul. Sure enough, he had become a 'real' Christian, with a personal faith. He was the first man I ever baptised by immersion in water (my own wife was the first woman, a few minutes earlier).

I asked him to 'give his testimony' (i.e. tell the story of his conversion) from the pulpit and this is exactly what he said:

"I believe in God the Father almighty, maker of heaven and earth. And in Jesus Christ, his only Son our Lord, who was conceived by the Holy Spirit, born of the Virgin Mary, suffered under Pontius Pilate, was crucified, dead, and buried; he descended into hell; the third day he rose again from the dead; he ascended into heaven, and sitteth on the right hand of God the Father Almighty; from thence he shall come to judge the quick and the dead. I believe in the Holy Spirit; the holy catholic church; the communion of saints; the forgiveness of sins; the resurrection of the body; and the life everlasting; Amen."

Reg then paused and added, "As a cathedral choirboy I recited those words every week, but they did not mean anything to me. Now I really believe them." And with that, he sat down. The atmosphere was electric. All of us felt twinges of guilt as we recalled words said, or more frequently sung, in church which we really did not mean, or even understand.

He was repeating the words of what has become known as 'the Apostles' Creed'. It is one of a number of such summaries of the Christian faith used in public worship to remind worshippers of what they have accepted as truth. Called 'creeds' because of their first word in their original language, Latin: *credo* means 'I believe'. In spite of the first person singular, they were intended for corporate recitation as well as private meditation. They functioned positively to confirm truth and negatively to contradict error.

The Apostles' Creed was one of the earliest 'confessions'.

It may not have been composed by the Twelve but was generally accepted as a précis of their teaching. The other well-known creed, the Nicene, is named after the city Nicaea, in what is now Turkey, where the Emperor Constantine held a council of churches to express the doctrinal unity of what had by then become different and even heretical streams of thought within Christian circles. It is much longer and more polemical, with terms taken from Greek philosophy. Jesus is described as 'God of God, Light of Light, very God of very God, begotten, not made, being of one substance with the Father....' Not surprisingly the earlier, simpler one has the wider appeal.

Both have three sections, corresponding to the three distinct persons within the Godhead: Father, Son and Holy Spirit. Without using the term 'Trinity', they nevertheless show that Christian faith was Trinitarian from the beginning. Years ago I wrote a hymn highlighting the differences between Christianity and Islam, set to the tune of *The Church's one Foundation*. The chorus after each verse ran:

> 'There is no God but Abba,
> And Jesus is his Son;
> Yet with the Holy Spirit,
> The Lord, our God is one.

The first two lines are a deliberate echo of and challenge to the Muslim creed ('There is no god but Allah and Mohamed is his prophet'). The last line quotes from the Jewish *Shema* from Deuteronomy 6:4 (in Hebrew the word for God, *Elohim*, is plural, meaning at least three, and the word for 'one' means to be 'in union', rather than 'singular', as in Adam and Eve becoming one flesh). The chorus, like the Creeds, is Trinitarian, without using the word 'Trinity' (which means tri-unity).

This book explores the middle section of the Apostles' Creed, hopefully with some fresh insights into its quite extraordinary claims about the Second Person of the Trinity. This is the longest of the three sections and is the heart of the Christian faith. 'Christianity is Christ' is a cliché that has been used so often that it is in danger of losing its impact. But it is still the truth and always will be. The focal point of all Christian thought is to be found in a person. 'What do you think about Christ?' (Matthew 22:42) is the most important question anybody could ever be asked; their eternal destiny depends on their answer.

Only if we realise who he *is* will we be able to appreciate what he has *done*. So the section begins with a fourfold statement about his person before describing his work. So we may say that a Christian is someone who has come to recognise these four features in this one person: 'Jesus Christ, his only Son, our Lord.'

First, his *humanity*. He was a real human being, living in our world. Very few doubt his existence. The name 'Jesus' was given to him when he was born and it is the name by which he is now world-famous. It was quite a common name (there are others in the New Testament: Colossians 4:11). In his own language, Hebrew, it is pronounced *Yeshua*, the same as 'Joshua' in the Old Testament. It means 'God saves' (the proprietor of our village post office in Hampshire is Mr. Godsave).

Second, his *royalty*. 'Christ' is not his surname. It is

not a name at all, but a title. It means 'anointed one', an epithet applied to prophets and priests in the Old Testament, but supremely to kings. The 'chrism', anointing with oil, was part of the coronation ceremony (as it is to this day, in Westminster Cathedral when British sovereigns are crowned). The Greek *Christus* is equivalent to the Hebrew *meschiah* (English 'Messiah'). Jesus was born and died 'King of the Jews' (Matthew 2:2; 27:37). He had royal blood in his veins, being a physical descendant of King David on his mother's side (Luke 3) and a legal one on his stepfather's (Matthew 1). It would be more meaningful to call him King Jesus than Jesus Christ. Above all, the title ties him to the Jewish race, which is why their scriptures (which they call 'the Ta'anach', but we call 'the Old Testament') are part of our Bible.

Third, his *divinity*. God was his Father. He always was and always will be. 'Only' points to a unique relationship between them. Jesus was the only one of his kind, the only 'natural' (the meaning of 'begotten') progeny of God. Human beings can join this tight-knit family, but only by adoption. Nor must we imagine that God was once all on his own and then produced a son like himself. The Father-Son relationship was never the result of sexual intercourse, as Muslims mistakenly believe; it was eternal. Always there. That is why Christians can say 'God *is* love'. 'He' was always persons in relationship. And all that the Father was could be seen in his Son (John 14:9, Colossians 1:19).

Fourth, his *authority*. The very earliest and shortest Christian 'creed' consisted of just three words: 'Jesus is Lord' (1 Corinthians 12:3). Later, to say that publicly could cost them their lives in an empire ruled over by a man claiming that title for himself, by implication also claiming a divine prerogative. To proclaim Jesus as 'Lord' was to be charged with treason, punishable by death. It was a title given to Jesus after he had been crucified and raised, then given a throne in heaven with supreme power and authority over the whole universe (Matthew 28:18; Philippians 2:9-11). In saying: '*our* Lord', Christians are acknowledging his headship over them, both individually and collectively.

These four attributes form the bedrock-foundation for everything else we know about him. It was so with his first followers. Only when they realised who he was could he really get on with what he had come to do for them (Mark 8:27-31). So with this initial statement in our minds we can turn to the extraordinary series of events which the authors of the Creed considered essential to Christian faith.

I have called them 'The Seven Wonders of His Story' because they are unique. They only happened once in the whole of human history and they all happened to this one person. What a story!

And it is all true. The first thing that strikes us is that they are presented as hard, *historical* facts. There are no embellishing adjectives, just basic phrases with verbs and subjects. There is no appeal to emotions. Christianity is a matter of facts, not feelings. Faith has a very solid foundation or it will fall when shaken.

Of course, faith must accept the facts as true. But it is not blind or unquestioning. It is supported by the very same kind of evidence which can persuade any court jury an event has occurred 'beyond reasonable doubt', namely a combination of eyewitness testimony and circumstantial evidence, both of which we have in abundance for Jesus Christ, compared with far less for Julius Caesar, for example. Ultimately, of course, whether we are willing to believe is a matter of personal choice.

Of the seven events, five are already past and two are future. But to believe the five and doubt the two would seem inconsistent and even irrational. Of the 737 predictions recorded in the Bible, 596 (81%) have already literally come true; it doesn't require great faith to believe that the rest will follow. We may add that to deny any one or even more of the seven is to fall short of full Christian faith. The well-known case of a bishop who refused to accept both the virgin birth and the bodily resurrection springs to mind, though he did not hesitate to recite the Apostles' Creed when worshipping!

The next thing to strike us is that these are largely *physical* facts, relating to Jesus' body rather than his soul. His conception, birth, suffering, burial, resurrection, even his ascension and return, are all 'in the flesh'. No wonder a former Archbishop of Canterbury (William Temple) said that Christianity is 'the most materialistic of all the world's religions'. That is why the Apostles' Creed goes on to say in its third section: 'I believe in… the resurrection of the body', rather than 'the immortality of the soul'. It is also why Paul talks about mortal souls putting on immortal bodies (1 Corinthians 15:53-55).

The third surprising feature is the somewhat *passive* part played by Jesus, at least in the past five events, which consist of things done for or to him rather than by him. He was conceived by the Holy Spirit, birthed by Mary, made to suffer by Pilate, crucified by Roman soldiers, buried by Joseph and Nicodemus, raised to life by God himself, taken up to heaven in a cloud. To think he did nothing himself would be a terrible mistake. He not only allowed it all to happen, he chose to let them all do it. Every act was voluntary on his part. He chose to be born, which no-one else has done or will ever do. He chose to die prematurely, even when, where and how to die. It was not just putting himself in the hands of others but in everything submitting to his Father's will: 'not my will but yours be done' (Mark 14:36).

One cannot help but notice the *omissions* in this creed. There is nothing between his birth and his death. There is no mention of his baptism at thirty, or of the temptations which followed. Not a word about his three years of public ministry. Neither the message he preached nor the miracles he performed. Why not? Quite simply, creeds focus on those key points essential to faith. The beginning and end of his life story are more significant than anything in between. Jesus was born to die. In theological terms, incarnation and atonement belong together. Paul defined the most important parts of the gospel as the death, burial and resurrection of Jesus. (1Corinthians 15:3-4). One third of all four Gospels is devoted to his death.

The major omission is any *explanation*. It is a list of what happened but no hint of why any of it happened. Perhaps this is why the later 'Nicene' creed said that Jesus 'came down from heaven... and was made man... for us men and for our salvation'. In this book I am exploring in more detail both the events themselves and their significance, what really took place and how it all fits into God's overall plan and purpose.

Finally, by way of introduction, a word of explanation and some personal comments. The following chapters are based on transcripts of a series of talks given to a huge crowd of young people at the International House of Prayer in Kansas City, Missouri, USA. They were most responsive, rounding off each session with clapping, cheering, whistling and 'tweeting' pithy comments on the internet, even while I was speaking ('This cute old English gentleman'). The talks were broadcast on the Internet and can still be viewed under 'IHOP'.

My spoken style, therefore, peeps through the written word from time to time — direct address, rhetorical questions, repetition, etc. Hopefully this will help the reader to be involved rather than distracted.

I am now eighty-two years of age (a member of the Israeli Knesset recently told me I didn't look a day over eighty!). So I am aware that each book I write could be my final publication. Since many have regarded some of my teaching (on male leadership, hell, baptism in the Spirit, pre-millennialism, Israel's future, etc.) as out of tune with much contemporary evangelicalism, I wanted, before I go to my eternal destiny, to show that I am sound as a bell on the fundamental facts of the faith. So here they are!

As always, I ask the reader to compare everything I say or write with what is written in the Bible and, if at any point a conflict is found, always to rely upon the clear teaching of scripture.

J. David Pawson

P.S. I am very grateful to a student at IHOP University, Erica Grimaldi, and her team for transcribing them for me, and to Peter and Justin Byron-Davies, my editors, who have skilfully turned my spoken words into this book.

1

The wonder of his BIRTH

Our faith as expressed in the Apostles' Creed is a very physical faith. Jesus was born, he was killed, he was buried, he was raised and it is all to do with his body. So not only is our faith based on fact, it's based on *physical* facts. That is good, isn't it? We are not one of these religions that is up in the clouds; our faith is very 'down to earth'.

The facts affirmed in the Creed were things that happened *to* Jesus or that were about him, not things that he did or said. He was conceived, he was born, he was crucified, he was buried, and he was raised. That can be a surprise for some. The next big surprise about the Apostles' Creed is how much is missed out: there is nothing about his baptism, teaching and miracles. It is a very incomplete account, but without these physical facts our faith would collapse. They are the foundation for our faith.

So we begin with the conception and birth of Jesus. He was **conceived by the Holy Spirit** and **born of the Virgin Mary**. Surprisingly, I am going to start with his birth and then move to his conception, which is far more important than his birth. Why do we make such a song and dance about his birth, yet make so little of his conception? I don't know, because the miracle happened at his conception. His birth was relatively normal, but his conception was unique and was the first wonder of 'His Story' we are thinking about.

THE BIRTH OF JESUS

No other birth in history is as widely celebrated as that of Jesus. Christmas is an almost universal phenomenon now, and in commerce Christmas begins about the middle of August. The shops begin to advertise that there are only so many shopping days till Christmas. They put the decorations up and begin to get the street lights ready. Especially in the Western world, Christmas is the biggest thing in the year for some communities. His birth is perhaps the most widely known event of Jesus' life, though it took place thousands of miles away from where many of us live. It was two thousand years ago — and we are still spending weeks celebrating it and a whole lot of money.

At first sight it was a very ordinary birth and quite an ordinary situation. So we begin by going through the human side of the story. We often neglect the human side of scripture, but we will be focusing on it because the Bible is both human and a divine book. When we separate out the human story, it is really not all that unusual. It is the story of a young Jewish couple in their teens and they have got married in a hurry because she was pregnant before the marriage — what is called a 'shotgun wedding' in some circles. By the time the baby came, they were very far from home, having travelled a long way.

Whatever has made a pregnant young woman travel mile after mile on a donkey? It is not the best thing for a pregnant woman to do. The answer is that, in her culture, premarital pregnancy was severely frowned upon. Indeed, it could be met with a death penalty, but she is away from her own culture because no one would look after her except her new husband. She has had to accompany him, because an emperor a thousand miles away has ordained a new tax and insisted on registering every citizen. They must go to their ancestral home to be registered, so they registered with their relatives. Therefore this young Jewish man was with his young wife, who was probably fifteen years of age, and he might have been seventeen or eighteen – that would be the usual age for such a couple – and they had to set off on a seventy mile journey to the place of registration. Had she been left at home, no one would have looked after her. They have reached the ancestral home town of Bethlehem, and it is now full of their relatives who have had to travel to the same place, but none of them is going to look after the young girl.

So they have gone to the public inn to get a place to sleep. To understand what happened you have to know what an inn was like in the Middle East. I want you to imagine a very high wall with no windows, in the form of a huge square. In that square wall, there is only one opening, a double gate under an archway in the front and then you are in. It is designed to protect travellers and their animals from bandits or marauders of any kind overnight. When you enter through the double gate, you see that all around the walls are individual rooms, sometimes on two storeys, and all the windows of the rooms face inward. You would ask, "Is there a room in the inn?" They were told there was no room, but that doesn't mean no space, it means no room for rent—however the courtyard in the middle has a well to provide water for the people and their animals, and there were troughs for the animal feed. The people book a room and leave their camels and donkeys in the courtyard, tying them up to posts, and feeding and watering them there. If you cannot get a room, then the only alternative is to camp in the courtyard with the animals. That was what this young couple had to do — bed down for the night in the courtyard among the animals, open to the sky.

After some hours in labour, this young girl, called after Moses' sister, in English 'Mary', in Hebrew 'Miriam', brought a little boy into the world. Having wrapped him in 'swaddling clothes' (but you can call them diapers if you like; we call them 'nappies' in England), she laid him in one of the feeding troughs. That is the picture you should have in your mind, not a stable. The Bible doesn't mention a stable and it certainly doesn't mention a cave. It just says that there was no room at the inn and she bore her baby and laid him in a manger. Not a very salubrious environment to give birth to a baby. Would you like your baby to be born in a cowshed? That's the nearest I think I can get to the situation, and that is what happened.

When a baby is born, you get visitors who must come and see him. The interesting thing is there is no record of any relatives coming to see this new baby, yet the town would have been full of their relatives – cousins, aunts and uncles. However, the baby does get visitors—two groups in fact: one very poor and the other very rich, one group of people who worked with their hands and the other group who worked with their heads. One group came only a few hundred yards, the other group came from many miles away to see the baby. The first group were nearby shepherds, who were among the poorest citizens in their culture in those days.

Do you remember that David's father presented his sons to
Samuel·Saul the prophet to be anointed as king? He presented all
his sons and Samuel said, "None of these. Don't you have
any more boys?" "Oh," he said, "Only the shepherd, the
youngest, David, he's out with the sheep. You can't mean
him." Shepherds were despised, they were the bottom of the
social ladder, but a group of them came to see the baby—they
were the first.

Then, some months later, some scholars came from a far
off country and said, "We want to see the baby." They had
brought very expensive gifts of gold, frankincense and myrrh
because they believed the baby had royal blood. Indeed he
had, because Mary and Joseph had come to Bethlehem, their
ancestral home, because they were descended from David.
So they had come to David's town, but the scholars who
came from a long way away didn't make for Bethlehem,
they made for Jerusalem. Somebody born to be a king is
going to be born in the capital.

Then, they gave the game away to the king called Herod
and he was not even a Jew. He was descended from Esau,
not Jacob. He was an Edomite and he had paid the Romans
who gave him the throne of Israel. Herod sat on that throne
and these innocent scholars came and said, "Where is the
King of the Jews born?" Herod was jealous and said, "As
soon as you find the boy, come and tell me where he is, that
I may come and worship him." Actually, what he meant in
his heart was, "That I may come and kill him." When those
wise men went home on a different route and didn't call at
Jerusalem to tell him where the baby was, Herod ordered
every boy under two in Bethlehem to be killed, for this
was some months after the birth. There was an almighty

slaughter and you realise that many of those babies killed were Jesus' relatives.

So Jesus' birth left many bereaved families. That is something you never see on a Christmas card, but it is part of the story. Joseph and Mary, the two young Jewish parents, had escaped just in time and became refugees hundreds of miles away, out of their own country. The first few years of the boy's life were in a different culture, a different language, until they managed to return later to their own village up north, in Nazareth, when Herod had died. Now, all that is the human side of the account, and it is all that the world believes.

Unbelievers have difficulty with the rest of the story. Even though they celebrate in school with nativity plays and celebrate Christmas and indulge in it all, that is as far as unbelievers will go with the whole story—but it is not the whole story. In fact, we have to go back over it and point out how many times a supernatural thing happened that made it possible. That whole sequence of events could not have taken place unless God had stepped in at crucial points and done or said something that changed the whole course of things. It is a romantic, fascinating story, but unless you believe in the supernatural and believe in God's intervention, you cannot understand it.

Before we look at the supernatural side of the record of those events, I want to trace it through from then until now at the human level and ask: Why has Christmas become what Christmas is at the human level? Why do we celebrate it so widely? I must give you a little history for that because it is an extraordinary story. In the northern hemisphere there were fertility cults, which were the pagan religions before

Christianity. The pagan religions were fertility cults, based on the idea of fertility and the vital fact of reproduction which, of course, is right at the heart of our natural life. Long before Christ came, in the northern hemisphere, in Europe, there was an annual festival on 25th December. It was held to celebrate the 'rebirth' of the sun on which our crops and everything else depended. The shortest day, the day of the sun's 'death' if you like, was on 21st December. Gradually the sun had been giving less and less light until that point in the year.

So they waited just a few days to make sure the sun had been reborn and then they celebrated that. The Roman world called the sun deity *Mithras*. So 25th December was the birthday of the 'sun god', and boy did they celebrate it! They celebrated with overeating, over drinking, and over sexing. It was a very indulgent festival. Does this strike a familiar note with you? They had songs, carols to celebrate the sun being born again. They had bonfires. They would cut down a big tree which they called the *yule* log and they burnt it. They would celebrate with evergreen trees because they thought the deciduous trees, which renew their leaves, are coming back with the sun — so they would take an evergreen tree and celebrate the birthday of the sun with it. Did you know that is where the Christmas tree came from?

Most of what we do at Christmas goes back to the fertility cults and pre-Christian pagan religion. Yet we think it is Christian! One other thing, which I hesitate to mention, is that the celebration lasted twelve days. Have you heard a song called *On the Twelve Days of Christmas My True Love Said to Me*? Why 'My true love'? Because each community elected one man to be 'lord of the festival'. For twelve days, he had the doubtful privilege of being able to sleep with any girl or woman in that community. For twelve days he celebrated. All that is thoroughly pagan and it was practised all over northern Europe long before Christ was born. When a Pope sent the first missionary to England, he landed in a town called Canterbury. He began to convert the people of the county of Kent, which was then the kingdom of Kent—even managing to convert the king, whom he baptised. But when he reported back to the Pope he said, "Sadly, I have not been able to take from the British people their mid-winter festival. It's a terrible pagan fertility cult, and they're so fond of it, I can't get them to drop it." So, the Pope said something which has been Roman Catholic missionary policy ever since: "Well don't try and stop them doing it, baptise it into Christ; bring it in." If you can't lick them, join them — that was his policy.

So all that came into the Christian faith in England, as the result of the Pope's decision, and became 'Christ-mass'. Because, on the morning of the birthday of the sun, he said, "You must celebrate the Son that is risen with healing in his wings, and come to mass." The word 'Christmas' tells you straight away of the Roman Catholic origin of the festival. That was what they did, and I am sorry to say, they are still doing it in territories such as South America and the Philippines. When I went to the Philippines, I was told they are all Catholics now — but they were still practising spiritism and animism. I thought, "How can you do that as a Christian?" but it was part of this policy of bringing existing culture into Christ, hoping to blend the two in a new, more healthy way. I am not surprised that Christmas in my country is rapidly going back to its pagan roots because that is what godless people enjoy, and it is losing its Christian content.

That is one of the great developments that has happened in the Western world, making Christmas such a commercial opportunity, such an indulgent season when we eat too much and drink too much and spend too much. It goes back to that Pope many centuries ago.

There have been other additions to the Christmas story. One comes from Turkey, where there was a Christian bishop by the name of Nicholas. Bishop Nicholas was a very sensitive man who felt for people and their needs, and in his diocese there was a poor man with three daughters. Alas, those three daughters could not marry. They were very attractive girls, but I'm afraid he couldn't get them married because in those days, the father of the bride had to provide a financial sum called a dowry to get his girls married. This poor man hadn't any money. The bishop heard about this, and secretly, one night he put some gold coins in a bag and somehow smuggled the bag into the poor man's cottage, though I don't think he put them in a stocking and I don't think he dropped it down the chimney!

The poor father was so excited because he could now marry off his three daughters and pay the dowry. Bishop Nicholas became 'Saint Nicholas', only they didn't say, "Nicholas" then. They said, "Nicholaus"— he became known as Santa Claus. Are you beginning to think things? That's the origin of Santa Claus and hanging up your stocking and Santa Claus coming down the chimney with presents for you. Once again, the Christmas story has got mixed up with other things. Oh, it's such a mixture! I have to say that it was America that invented 'Father Christmas' with his red robes (with cotton wool nowadays, but ermine originally). Father Christmas was a North American figment of the imagination that has been added. As for Rudolf the red-nosed reindeer, I don't know where he came from—probably Scandinavia.

There came a day in our home, when my young son said to me, "Daddy, is there a Father Christmas?" I said, "No, son. It's a made-up story that we like to believe." He went straight to the kitchen, to his mother, and said, "Mummy, Daddy doesn't tell the truth." I was in the doghouse a whole year before he discovered that I told him the truth because I will not tell a lie to a child. If they ask a question, I will tell them the true answer. I think pretending things to them that they will discover are not true can be very damaging to your relationship.

So there it is. Christmas has become this incredible mixture of truth and fiction. Of course, since we love a story, even embellishments to the original story have been mixed into it. For example: the idea that there were *three* wise men. The Bible doesn't say that—it's all due to having brought three gifts. I have watched a few school nativity plays and they really are so funny, when the children get it all wrong. I remember one nativity play where a little boy came on and said, "Here is gold for the baby Jesus." The second boy came on and said, "Here is myrrh for the baby Jesus." The third boy came on and said, "Frank sent this." In another school play which was equally funny (sorry, it's my sense of humor running away with me again), Joseph and Mary turned up at the inn, knocked at the door, and when the innkeeper came, they said, "Have you got a room for us?" The innkeeper said, "Of course I have. Come on in. You can have the best room in the inn" and there was *ad libbing* galore. Happily, the boy playing Joseph had a quick mind and he stuck his head through the door, then turned to Mary and said, "You should see the state of the room in there." He said, "We'd be better off in the stable, come on" — and rescued the play.

But not only do we think there were three wise men, we think they were kings — *We Three Kings from Orient Are*. They weren't three kings at all. We've even given them names. Perhaps worst of all, we have called them Gentiles because we Gentiles wanted to be in the Christmas story. It was all Jewish — surely the Gentiles had some place in it? But they were Jewish wise men who had stayed behind in Babylon when other Jews had returned to their own land. (We will return to that.)

Well, there it is, we are lumbered with Christmas. I'm afraid I'm preaching and telling people, "Get Christ out of Christmas." Celebrate his birth when he was born; he certainly wasn't born in December. Shepherds don't watch their flocks by night in December. It's cold in them there hills in December! He was born, according to my Bible, at the end of September/beginning of October, during the Feast of Tabernacles. Let me give you the biblical basis for that. It is found in Luke's Gospel with a sequence of events before he was born, which went something like this: John the Baptist's father, Zechariah, went into the temple to pray. One of his burdens was that his wife Elizabeth was barren and had never presented him with a child. He was praying and he was told, "Your wife will bear a son."

I am quite sure that when he got home, he hardly had his supper before he took her to bed. She conceived and John was born but, when she was six months pregnant, the same angel that had spoken to her went and spoke to Mary and

27

said, "You are going to have a son, and if you want proof go and visit your cousin Elizabeth because she is having a baby." So Mary went to visit Elizabeth in her sixth month and Jesus was born nine months later. That's a total of fifteen months (six months pregnancy for Elizabeth and nine months pregnancy for Mary). If we knew when Zechariah went into the temple to pray, fifteen months later would be the date of Jesus' birth. A bit mathematical, but I think you will be able to add up the figures! We do know when Zechariah went in and which house of priests he belonged to. The houses of priests took two weeks in the temple in turn; his house was in the third month. We know that from the Old Testament where the houses of the priests are listed in Chronicles. So we now know the fifteen months come to the seventh month of the next year. That is when Jesus was born, in the Feast of Tabernacles, and that is where the scripture had always promised the Messiah would appear. You will find that in Zechariah, the prophet.

So, if you want to celebrate Jesus' birth, do it at the end of September or beginning of October. You will find it is much cheaper and simpler. Blaming Jesus for all that we spend and eat and drink, frankly I just think is not Christian. So, I am encouraging Christians not to observe Christmas as a 'Christ event'. Celebrate it as a family thing if you want to. Let us preach Christ when he was born and focus on him without all the razzmatazz around it. Sorry, that's one of the bees in my bonnet!

Let's go back to the original text: let's go back to the supernatural part. Journey backwards in the account and see how many times you can't explain what happened without God—right back to the beginning. For one thing, you can't explain the story without angels, and angels are a real part of God's creation. We are not the peak of God's creation, angels are above us. God has made us humans a little lower than the angels and above the animals. We are not animals, we are not angels — we are in between. That is the biblical place for human beings. If we think we are the top, we forget who we are and we become proud, thinking, "Boy, we're the tops," but we are not, we are second. Angels are the top creatures, we are the second and animals are the third, and you must never get those three mixed up if you are going to understand the truth about the human race. That is why, for example, the Bible forbids sexual relations between those three. We are to have sexual relations with human beings, not with animals, though that has always been part of perverted humanity. We are not to have sex with angels because that is what led to all the trouble before Noah's flood. That is what introduced occultism into the human race. That is what introduced kinky sex and violence to the human race — when angels and human beings had sex. God wants us to stay within our status and acknowledge that there are creatures above us and creatures below us. Then, we can get a right perspective on ourselves and human pride would not put itself at the top. That is a very important thing, but you know, even in school nativity plays, they always have angels and stick cardboard wings on the backs of the children, but they don't really believe it. They think it is like fairies at the bottom of your garden. Angels are not fairies; angels are more intelligent than we are. They are able to move more quickly than we can. They are more attractive to look at than we are. They are above us in the order of creation.

Angels play a crucial part in the events surrounding our

Lord's birth. Without them it would not have happened. Angels play a significant role all the way through Jesus' life. You find that at every critical point angels are involved. So, if you don't believe in angels, you will not believe in the accounts of the life of Jesus recorded in the Gospels — you cannot. They were there in the wilderness when he was tempted. They were there in the garden of Gethsemane when he was in such agony. The only crisis they were not present at was his death, but they were there again at his resurrection, and again at his ascension. If you don't believe in angels then the story makes nonsense; but they are God's messengers.

The whole story began with an angel, Gabriel, who appeared to Mary and told her the most remarkable thing: "God wants to make you pregnant." What a message! No woman before Mary had ever heard such a message, and she believed it. Yes, she had a bit of discussion with the angel. She said, "How can I have a baby? I haven't known a man. I've never had sex; I'm a virgin." Then she was told, "God will make you pregnant. He will do it inside you and you will have a son." What an announcement! They call it officially in some church circles, the 'Annunciation'. It took that fifteen year old village girl and made her very special. God didn't choose her *because* she was special; by choosing her he made her special.

Because Roman Catholics make too much of Mary, Protestants make too little by reaction. I have heard so many sermons on the great heroes and heroines of the Bible but I have never yet heard an Evangelical preach on Mary. I have done it myself. I spoke to a group of Roman Catholic priests, with a Roman Catholic cardinal sitting three feet in front of me. I said, "I want to tell you what the Bible does say about Mary and what it doesn't say about Mary." Pretty bold, I'm afraid! The cardinal came to me afterwards and said, "I sure pray that 'Our Lady' will appear to you." I've met him a few times since and say to him, "She hasn't yet."

The Bible says some wonderful things about Mary. She was the first Charismatic in the New Testament. She said, "Let the Holy Spirit do with me what you want." What an amazing thing. She spoke in tongues, but not until the day of Pentecost. She was among the hundred and twenty who were baptised in the Holy Spirit and spoke in tongues. But from then on she disappeared. She became a member of the congregation. Her work was done. She quietly and modestly retired into the fellowship of believers. It is an amazing story. Right through her life, Jesus was dissociating himself from her. At the first miracle, changing water into wine at Cana, he did not call her 'Mother', he said, "Woman, what have I to do with you?" When they came later and said, "Jesus, your mother and brothers and sisters are outside and they have come to take you home — they seem to think you are beside yourself, schizophrenic," he said, "Who is my mother? Who are my brothers? Whoever does the will of my Father in heaven is my mother." On the cross he called his beloved disciple John to the foot of the cross where his mother was standing and said, "John, this is your mother from now on. Mary, John is your son", and handed her over to John.

We need to know what the Bible says is marvellous about Mary, and we need to be balanced and not say things about her that the Bible does not say. I think the world of Mary, but I think highly of Joseph. What a man! Only a young man, and when he found that his fiancé was pregnant he was shocked. Yet, he did not want to hurt her so he resolved to cancel the engagement, which in Jewish culture is like divorcing. He resolved to divorce her privately and dissociate himself from this pregnant teenager, but he did not do so. Like his namesake Joseph in the Old Testament, this young man was a dreamer and believed God could speak through dreams. He had a dream, and God said, "Don't worry about Mary being pregnant. She has not been unfaithful to you; she has not been playing around. I've done that." Joseph believed that. He was the first man to believe God could make a woman pregnant—what amazing faith! It says that as soon as he woke up after the dream, he married her. Therefore, he was taking the blame of the pregnancy on himself and society would blame him for anticipating the marriage. What a wonderful young man. Later, it was in a dream that God said, "Your baby is going to be killed unless you get him out of here quickly." As soon as he dreamt that, he believed it and he saved our Saviour for us and got him out of harm's way—what a wonderful man.

The angels were a vital part of the story. If you treat them like fairies, you miss the meaning. We asked how those two groups of visitors heard about the baby. It wasn't an announcement in the press; it wasn't cards sent everywhere announcing the baby's arrival. So how did they hear? The shepherds heard because the angels announced it. They were looking into the starry sky, and suddenly there were angels filling the sky, singing their heads off — an amazing, supernatural experience. Immediately, they left the sheep and headed off for the town. The angels even told them, "You will find him in an animal trough. Go and see him." With the wise men, it was even more supernatural—they saw a star.

Now, you must realize that back in the book of Numbers

there had been an amazing prophecy by a man called Balaam, whose donkey spoke to him—that was supernatural. He had predicted that the sceptre would arise in Judah and would be signalled by a star. Only Jews would know that prophecy; only Jewish wise men would be looking for it. When they saw a most unusual star, they decided to go home to Israel, for that is where they belong, and to see this King. They went to Jerusalem where they expected to find a royal prince, but they didn't find him there. As soon as they came out of Herod's palace, there was the star again, and just two miles south of Jerusalem is Bethlehem. It is an amazing story and they followed the star. There have been so many astronomical discussions of the star: was it three planets coming together, or three stars coalescing? We don't know. We just know that they knew that a star would mark the birth of the King of the Jews and they believed it. So, you get this remarkable combination of supernatural intervention and faith on the part of people believing what they were told. Without it we would not know what happened.

So Mary was a virgin right through her pregnancy and the birth of the baby. That is the first time it has happened as it did then, and the last. This is one of the 'wonders of his story' and it is the wonder of history as well.

Jesus was born to die and Mary knew it. She was told by a prophet that a sword would pierce her own heart. She had to live with that knowledge in her heart, not telling anyone — not even Joseph, apparently.

HIS CONCEPTION

The real miracle of our Lord's birth occurred nine months earlier. It therefore means that his conception happened during December — and probably 25th December. So, ironically, we may be celebrating his birth when we should be celebrating his conception because that is what really began it all. First, I want to ask: what exactly happened in Mary's womb? Of course no one could see it happening, but we now know so much about the beginning of life. We have so many facts available on our computers that we can begin to ask what really happened in Mary's body at the time of the conception.

What is a miracle? I define a miracle as *a natural event with a supernatural cause*. That covers every miracle I know. So let us ask: could there be a natural virgin birth? The answer is yes. I was discussing this with a professor of gynaecology in London University, and he said, "Yes, there could be." We know that there are instances in nature of a virgin birth among plants and even animals. A komodo dragon has had virgin births. What happens in such a birth is that the female egg is somehow stimulated to begin dividing without being fertilized, and it just goes on dividing until it has produced another individual. That professor also told me that he knew of six human cases which were possible virgin births, where in a woman's body the female ovum had spontaneously, without fertilization, begun to divide. Then the professor told me a most interesting thing. He said, "But, in every case it produced a baby girl, and that's because every egg in a woman's body is female. It has to be the male who changes that female egg into a male foetus." So even though it is possible that other women have had virgin births, it can never produce a baby boy — but Mary had a boy. That puts it in a category by itself. It is absolutely impossible for a female to produce male offspring by herself. Therefore, Mary does stand unique. God made her pregnant.

So what exactly did God do? There are three possibilities which we now know from our amazing new knowledge of the beginnings of life. They are these: first, that God created within her womb a fully fertilized egg from nothing. God creates from nothing; He could easily do that. Did he create a complete fertilized egg in her uterus? If that was what he did, then Mary would not be the mother of Jesus. She would be a surrogate mother—no more than an incubator—nursing that created egg. It would mean that Christ was not fully hers. It would mean that he was not Son of David, not Son of Abraham, not Son of Adam, but a totally new creature. Some people I meet believe that, but that would mean that Jesus was more divine than human. So I am ruling out that explanation.

The second possibility is that God took one of Mary's eggs and did some genetic modification to it. This theory says that all he needed to do was change the x-chromosome into a y-chromosome and that would have produced a baby boy. It is a very minor modification that was needed. However, if that was what he did there is now too much of Mary in the baby. The baby is virtually a clone of his mother except that his sex is different. Jesus would be an identical twin of Mary and would be more human than divine, more Son of

Man than Son of God. So I rule that out as well.

We are left with the only remaining possibility: that God created within Mary's womb a male sperm with all the DNA of the Son of God in it, and that that fertilized Mary's egg and produced Jesus, in which case Jesus would be equally divine and human. He would be Son of Mary and Son of God — Son of Man as well as Son of God —fully both, having a human mother and a divine Father. It's interesting that over the centuries of church history most heresies have denied one or the other of those facts, or both. There was one heresy called 'docetism' according to which it was believed that Jesus was fully divine but not fully human, only appearing to be a human. The very word 'docetism' means 'a mask', or appearing to be something you are not. At the opposite end there was another Christian heresy whose adherents believed he was fully human but never fully divine, but it seems to me that, right from the very beginning, the way he was conceived meant that Jesus was both fully human and fully divine—that is the full Christian truth.

As a human, he had a beginning. As a divine person, he had no beginning. Now I know this is getting into quite deep thinking, but this is my attempt to face the facts and to see what actually happened. It means that Jesus was both Creator and creature. If you deny either of those two truths you miss the essential truth about our Lord Jesus Christ. He was the Creator at the beginning and became a creature within his own creation. What an amazing thing to say. Before he ever made chairs and tables as a carpenter, he made the trees from which he got the wood. Before he ever preached the Sermon on the Mount, he made the mount so that he could have a pulpit. I am just spelling it out so that you begin to realize what an astonishing claim we are making for the person of our Lord Jesus Christ. Therefore, we have a problem when we want to tell someone the story of Jesus: where on earth are we going to begin?

Mark's Gospel begins with his baptism, when Jesus was thirty years old. Matthew's account of Jesus goes back to Abraham — in the very first page of Matthew we learn that he was son of Abraham. Luke takes the reader back to Adam. Finally, along came John who said that in the beginning he was already there. So we have a problem: where do we start when telling people about Jesus?

It is right not to overload people with the whole truth at the beginning. You can tell the story of Jesus from his birth onwards or from his maturity onwards—from thirty onwards. But the real story of Jesus begins right back, and John is consciously echoing Genesis, 'In the beginning God created the heavens and the earth.' He picks out that phrase, 'In the beginning'. He doesn't say, 'In the beginning he was,' but, 'In the beginning he was already there.' Our brains can't go back beyond the beginning of the universe; we just can't imagine nothing. So our brains can only go back to the beginning, and all the big debate about the 'Big Bang' is about the beginning. Scientists tend not to be discussing beyond that because our brain won't take in when there was nothing—not even space. So we have to go back to the beginning of the universe, and there he is already there.

Now when John wrote his Gospel after knowing Jesus for sixty years, he had a problem: what do you call Jesus before he was born? He thought up a brilliant answer, and he called him, in Greek, the *logos*. Now *logos*, among its other meanings, means 'word', and so he called him 'the Word'.

In the beginning was the Word or the *logos*, and the Word was with God face to face, and the Word was God. It is no wonder the Jehovah's Witnesses have had to change that wording in their Bible. Did you know they had? They cannot accept that Jesus was God. In fact, Jehovah's Witnesses are just one group that denies the full divinity of Jesus. They believe he was a creature of God but never the Creator. That heresy has come up in many different sects and groups, but we know better.

Now what does it mean to call Jesus the 'Word'? He was only called Jesus after he began as Son of Man. So what should you call him before? Now John wrote his Gospel in a town called Ephesus which is still there. It is one of the most impressive ruins in western Turkey; you must go and see it some day. There is still a magnificent public library, and they are now excavating the wealthiest homes on the hillside around it. It is a marvellous place to visit. When we went, I was making a film about the seven churches of Asia, and I got the cameraman to hire a small plane to take film of Ephesus from above. He duly took off and was flying over the ruins of Ephesus, and there was nobody there except one person, a lady, and around the edge of Ephesus were men with guns! The lady was Hillary Clinton and the guards were closing Ephesus off to everybody. My cameraman flew down over that scene with people ready with their guns, but he got some good shots. The one thing I wanted to see in Ephesus was the tomb of the apostle John. It is there; it is genuine. I remember standing at the tomb of the man who wrote the fourth Gospel, and I thanked the Lord for him and for all he wrote for us—wonderful stuff. Jesus loved him more than anybody. So he was in a position to tell us the inside story.

Matthew, Mark and Luke tell us the outside story, but John tells you the inside story. It is amazing. I am sure you have realised that John is so different from the other three Gospels.

So John writes, 'In the beginning was the Word'—the *logos*. Now why did he choose that? Because there was in Ephesus a Greek scientist called Heraclitus, and he was the man who invented science. He taught his students to observe and to analyse, and he said, "Study the weather, study the animals, observe everything in nature, and try and find the reason why it all happens as it does." He called the reason why the *logos*, and every branch of science is therefore called an 'ology'—whether it's zoology, psychology, sociology. Every branch of science is trying to find the reason why things work as they do. So science itself is dedicated to finding the *logos*. In choosing that word as the name of the pre-existent Jesus, John is saying, "He is the supreme reason why it is all here."

What scientists do is investigate part of the world around us. Astronomy looks at the stars, geology looks at the earth, but science becomes more and more specialised, scientists know more and more about less and less. It is homing in on things. But scientists don't stop to ask, 'What is the reason why the whole of nature operates as it does? Why is it all here?' What John is saying is, 'Jesus is why it's all here.' God made it all for Jesus. He is going to inherit it all, and we in Christ will inherit it with him. The meek shall inherit the earth. He is the reason why—I love that title for Jesus.

But the *logos* was taken from Ephesus across the Mediterranean to a city in Egypt called Alexandria where there was the greatest university in the ancient world after Athens. Its teaching was based on Greek philosophy. But to that university, just before Jesus' day came a Jewish philosopher called Philo. Philo in Alexandria took up this idea of the *logos*, took up the idea that the *logos* was involved in the creation and tended to make the *logos* the agent of God in creation and said that God created the world by the Word — again, the *logos* came in. So the word has a very interesting story, but it is saying that Jesus is the reason why everything happens as it does. It is saying that Jesus was there at creation, but he wasn't called Jesus then. That was only the name given to him for his supreme task on earth which was to deliver his people from their sins. So he should be called Jesus because that means 'God saves'.

In the little village where we live there is a post office and the postman is called 'Mr Godsave'. We go and see 'Mr Godsave' the postman regularly. That little name 'God Save' is an exact English equivalent to *Yesous* in Greek or *Yeshua* in Hebrew—God saves. Well now, when he was creating the universe, God and Jesus and the Holy Spirit were not aiming to redeem the world from sin. That came later, but when it came, the *logos* was a very good word to use. What John is saying is that Jesus existed long before he was born, but he was not known by that name. That was the name of the Son of Man who did begin at his conception, but it's not the name of the Son of God who was always there. Again, I hope your mind is beginning to burst because these are amazing truths at the heart of scripture. If we once lose the faith that Jesus is fully God and fully man, something will go terribly wrong with our faith.

It means, to put it as simply as I can, that Jesus was and still is the only human being who chose to be born. You and I did not choose to be born. We did not choose our parents or the social status into which we would be brought up. Jesus chose his own very humble parents. He could have chosen to be born in the most expensive palace in the world, but he chose to be born in the home of a working man, a carpenter—the humility of it!

Philippians chapter 2 describes his choices as humble all the way. He was equal with God, and he chose to be a man. He was equal to men, but he chose to be a servant. Then the ultimate choice was that he chose to die at the age of thirty-three. Very few people do that deliberately. Even soldiers, who know they can be killed, hope not to be. They don't deliberately go to war to be killed. They know they may be, and that is quite a choice—but the ultimate choice is to choose certain death. That is unusual.

So Jesus chose to be born. I once tried with my three children to get this across to them. We had a tank of tropical fish, and there was one fish that spoiled the whole tank. It was always attacking the others and eating them. The poor children had to watch this. I took them to the front of the fish tank and said, "Supposing you could stop all that happening in that fish tank, if you were willing to become a fish, and I popped you in there, in the fish tank, to stop all the fighting, knowing that they might turn on you and kill you—would you be willing to do that?" My three little children were horrified, "Never!" But I said, "What if you did that and I picked you out of the fish tank and brought you back, and you had to stay a fish for the rest of your life," and that horrified them even more. You know, Jesus didn't become a man for thirty-three years and then go back to being God. He became a man forever; he is still a man. He became one of us for the rest of eternity.

I was talking to a dear Catholic lady, and I said to her, "Why do you pray to Mary?"

She said straight away, "Because she's human; she understands us."

I said, "But Jesus is human."

"Oh no, he's not. He was human, but he's now divine again in heaven."

I replied, "He's still a man," and I took her through the letter to the Hebrews which keeps emphasising he is a high priest in heaven who understands us — because he is still a man who was tempted like we are, and he still remembers that. He is a man in heaven. We have a human being in heaven, at the right hand of God who is running the universe now and who is above all the angels. He is therefore described as our pioneer. He is the first human being ever to get that high and to get above the angels and sit at the right hand of God. He has only done that so that one day we can do the same. So he is called our pioneer, our trailblazer, and the one who has gone ahead to prepare the way for us.

Our destiny is above the angels—that is where God has decided to place us, having redeemed us. We will sit with Christ in heavenly places and run the universe with Jesus. That is your future and I hope you are getting ready for it, not lording it over others but gaining the dignity of those who are going to reign with Christ.

'In the beginning was the Word' (John 1) tells us about Jesus' eternity. 'The Word was face-to-face with God'—that tells us about his deity, or rather his personality. The word is literally face-to-face with God, a personal relationship. So we have his eternity and his personality. Then, '... and the Word was God' tells us of his deity, his full divinity. Then a little further on in the chapter, the Word comes up again. John writes, 'And the Word became flesh and tabernacled among us'—or, translating it, 'and pitched his tent among us.' That is the most astonishing statement of all: the Word was eternal; the Word was personal; the Word was divine, and the Word became flesh. The word for *flesh* — 'carnal' — means 'fleshly'—and 'incarnation' means to 'come into flesh'. We must take the reality of that word seriously. What kind of flesh did Jesus enter? I give you a number of answers. First, it was *physical* flesh, not an appearance of flesh. You could touch and feel it. It was flesh like ours. You may feel this is irreverent, but I want to make my point: Jesus had to empty his bladder and bowels every day, just like me. We never think about such things, do we? Somehow we like him in a stained-glass window, above such earthly things. Jesus adopted our flesh. It would mean that he would be hungry and thirsty and tired and experience other things we experience. Really get a hold of this: the Word became flesh—physical flesh just like us.

In the Christmas carol *Away in a Manger* there is a lot that I refuse to sing. In fact, whenever I am in worship and something I don't believe in is sung, I don't sing. I wish everybody else would do the same. We would all go quiet now and again—and that would teach the songwriters something. In *Away in a Manger* is the line 'No crying he makes'. How utterly ridiculous—there is only one way a baby can tell the mother he is hungry and that is by crying! And have you noticed how Christmas cards show Jesus as a six-month old baby? He's always puffed-out and fully formed. When I first saw my first daughter, I was horrified. She looked like a skinned rabbit and I thought, "Did we produce that?" But you never see a Christmas card with a newborn baby lying in the manger, do you? He would have had to be washed and fed. His umbilical cord would have to be tied off. It is *physical* flesh that he became — one of us! Not in a stained-glass window but in real life. Thank God that his Son became one of us.

Secondly, it wasn't just physical flesh; it was *Jewish* flesh. Alas, the western world has forgotten that Jesus was, is, and always will be a Jew. He was circumcised on the eighth day like every Jewish baby boy. The church which forgets that Jesus is a Jew is going to get into difficulties. I have seen so many Sunday Bible school take-home papers for children which seem to suppose that Jesus is Scandinavian: flowing, fair hair, blue eyes. But he was a Middle-Eastern Jew – dark – and we forget that. We tend to make Jesus in our image because we like to think he is one of us. He was, but his was Jewish flesh; he had a Jewish nose; he was circumcised. So any anti-Semitism in the church is a gigantic denial of his Jewish flesh. Think that through for yourself.

Thirdly, it was *male* flesh. I am afraid the popular thing nowadays is to say that he was either bisexual or homosexual. That's a lie about our Jesus. He was born a man, he remained a man. Pontius Pilate said, "Behold, the man", even though feminism may try hard. There is a large Christian church in which there is a crucifix above the altar, and the figure of Jesus on the cross is totally naked and totally female. I am ashamed to say that sculpture was produced by Winston Churchill's granddaughter. Some of you may know the church where it is. That is a libel. Jesus was a man, male flesh, and we can never forget that because God is a Father, not a mother. He is the King of the universe, not a queen.

When Jesus came to show us what God is like, it had to be male flesh. I am spelling all this out because so often we have the wrong idea. It was physical flesh; it was Jewish flesh. It was male flesh, and it was sexual flesh.

Jesus was a normal male. Now there have been some abuses of that. For example, Scorsese's film *The Temptation of Christ* was abusing that, but it is still true. Jesus was a sexual being, bound to be. I thank him that he had the temptations I had as a male, and that he didn't give way to temptation. He was brought up a boy, then a man, and he knew sexual temptation among other temptations. That is part of belief in the Word become flesh. The *Da Vinci Code* has made out that he married Mary Magdalene and had a family. That is not true. But it is perfectly true that he could have married and could have had a family but chose not to.

Finally, and this may be the biggest shock to you of all: His flesh was *sinful flesh*—the Bible says that. Now that's something we cannot bear to think. So the Catholics have invented a doctrine called 'The Immaculate Conception of the Virgin Mary' and believe that Mary was born without sinful flesh. Now there is nothing of that in the Bible but most Protestants seem to believe in the Immaculate Conception of Jesus—that he wasn't born with sinful flesh but Paul says he was in Romans chapter 8. 'Born,' he says, 'in the likeness of sinful flesh.' Ah, says someone, only in the *likeness*.... Just a minute. In Philippians chapter 2, Paul says he was born in the likeness of man, so it doesn't just mean the outward appearance; it means the exact reproduction.

But surely Jesus was 'sinless' and needed to be in order to offer an atoning sacrifice for our sins. Perhaps we need to be reminded that temptation is not sin, even when it comes from within us. What we are saying is that Jesus inherited our fallen nature from his mother but never once gave way to it, living his whole life without sinning. This is a great encouragement to us in our battle with the world, the flesh and the devil. He has faced all three, been tempted in all points just as we are, yet without sin. That is why he is both a fully sympathetic high priest and also able, by his Spirit, to give us victory in daily living. He really did become one of us and yet is not like any one of us in resisting all temptations successfully.

So, 'He was born in the likeness of sinful flesh' which means that Jesus was tempted, not just from the outside by the world and the devil but from the inside by his flesh. I am thankful for that and I say it reverently, but it means that Jesus has fought all my battles and has been through it all himself, yet without sin. He has done it all and if he can conquer the world, the flesh, and the devil, then by his strength and grace I can, too—that is the good news, but people think he was born with no trace of sinful flesh. He inherited that from Mary. She was a sinful woman like all of us; it was the grace of God that made her what she was. Her son was born in the likeness of sinful flesh and gained a victory even over that. Thank you, Jesus! Thank you for doing all that for me.

Well, he chose to be born; he chose to be flesh. It was a voluntary act and a very humbling act to do it not just for a short period but forever. Now we must grasp the deepest truth of all in his conception. What was it? Well, it was that he was not just bringing divinity into humanity—that's wonderful enough because then he can say to people, "If you have seen me, you have seen the Father." If you want to know what God is like, then look at Jesus. He's a chip off the old block. He is, really — he looks like his Father. So, he brought divinity into humanity. That is one side of it that we have little difficulty believing and which we often think about, but the other side of it we tend to neglect. The other side is that he took humanity into divinity. That is the revolution that happened when Jesus was conceived — our humanity was taken into divinity. I find that almost too much to imagine — it is breathtaking. But now one of the three persons of the godhead is human. Isn't that an amazing truth? If you have never thought about it before, go on thinking about it.

So finally, I ask: why did he do all this? Why was he willing to do it, voluntarily doing it for me and for you and for the whole world — even for the whole universe? Why was the Creator willing to become a creature? The twofold answer is very simple: to bring God to us and to bring us to God. The Bible talks about both things. He did it to bring God to us so that we would know that God was one of us, and to bring us to God, that we might be his adopted sons. Jesus is the only begotten Son, but we are adopted sons and daughters, adopted into his family forever.

The Apostles' Creed jumps straight from Jesus' birth to his death. It is an extraordinary jump, and yet it was his death more than anything else that brings us back to God — makes it all possible. Not long after his birth they took him two miles away to the temple, to be dedicated and circumcised. It was then that they met two lovely people, a woman called Anna and a man called Simeon. It was Simeon who prophesied to Mary, "This child of yours will be the means of saving Israel, but it will pierce your own heart with a spear." Then he said a wonderful thing: "Lord, I can die happy! I've seen him!" Here was a man who had waited all his life but knew God had told him, "Before you die you'll see the King; you will see my Son." Now Simeon says, "Lord, now let your servant depart in peace. I can die happy." All he had seen was a little baby but such was his faith that he could see what that baby would become for Israel and for the Gentile world—for all of us.

*****

There are plenty of Christmas carols and some of them are pretty mushy, but I want to refer here to a really good hymn by Charles Wesley, who in my judgment is the greatest hymn writer there has ever been. He wrote six thousand hymns. Alas, only a few are sung today, though they are packed with the most amazing thoughts about the Lord.

> Glory be to God on high,
> and peace on earth descend!
> God comes down,
> He bows the sky,
> and shows Himself our friend:
> God the invisible appears!
> God the blessed, the great I AM
> sojourns in this vale of tears,
> and Jesus is His name.

Him the angels all adored,
their Maker and their King.
Tidings of their humbled Lord
they now to shepherds bring.
Emptied of His majesty,
of His dazzling glories shorn,
being's source begins to be,
and God Himself is born!

See the eternal Son of God,
a mortal Son of Man;
dwelling in an earthly clod,
whom heaven cannot contain!
Stand amazed, ye heavens, at this!
See the Lord of earth and skies;
humbled to the dust He is,
and in a manger lies.

We, the sons of men, rejoice,
the Prince of Peace proclaim;
with heaven's hosts we lift our voice
and shout Immanuel's name:
knees and hearts to Him we bow;
of our flesh and of our bone,
Jesus is our brother now,
and God is all our own.

Isn't that a wonderful hymn? I hope some day you will be able to sing it, when you don't observe Christmas again!

2

The wonder of his
DEATH

Considering that Jesus is the most famous person who ever lived, we know surprisingly little about him. From his birth to the age of thirty, the curtain only lifts once for a brief glimpse of his boyhood, and then it falls again until he is thirty. The story of his birth is celebrated around the world every year, though treated by many as legend and myth, but the next thirty years are almost a complete blank, which is extraordinary. We assume that he joined his father in the family business of carpentry, making chairs and tables, doors and window frames. For those thirty years he was unknown and unnoticed and then suddenly at the age of thirty he strides out onto a very public stage and changes his career from woodworker to wonder worker—and it is interesting that he was a woodworker for eighteen years and a wonder worker for three. In my mathematics, that is six-to-one. Does that remind you of anything? Go and read Genesis chapter 1 again. Jesus said, "My Father works until now, and now I work."

He did have amazing powers which he only used for good to help people. He never used his power to hurt anyone, or as Peter later put it in a sermon, "He went about doing good." He helped people: the sick were healed, the blind saw, the deaf heard, the lame walked, the hungry were fed, and he even saved his disciples from drowning. He never did anything but good, yet three years later he was dead. That takes a lot of explaining.

Let us begin by thinking about the cross from the human side. There was a human story as well as a divine one. Just as with the birth, I tried to tell you the human story first and then the divine, I am going to do the same thing with his death.

So at thirty-three years of age, in the prime of life, less than half the average age expected in those days of seventy years, he was dead. Surprisingly, we know more about his death than his life. Isn't that extraordinary? He didn't die from natural causes, from sickness, old age or any other of those things which take us. He was murdered — a judicial, official murder. He was virtually assassinated—exterminated as a dangerous criminal, and all he had done was go around doing good for three years. He was considered the most dangerous man alive and therefore to be put to death as quickly as possible.

What explained that extraordinary reversal from being one of the most popular men of his day to being seen as one of the most dangerous? Most people know he was executed but they don't fully appreciate how he was put to death. There have been many forms of capital punishment: hanging has been quite popular, and the electric chair in America. In Rome they were often decapitated, their heads cut off with a sword. None of these things was the way Jesus died—for him was reserved the longest, most lingering, most humiliating, most painful death that has ever been devised for human beings. Capital punishment today tries to find ways of making it quick and painless; injections are now the popular way, but for Jesus it was just the opposite. I will go into the gory details later because I want you to realise what a dreadful death it actually was.

Crucifixion did not kill quickly—the shortest you could expect was two days on a cross, and the longest recorded is seven days. The condemned person was stripped naked. They were then nailed to two beams of wood through the wrists—not the palms of the hand, those would tear with the weight of the body. There is a hole in the wrist joint that they used to put the nails through, which could support the weight. The same with the feet: it was not through the middle of the feet but through the ankle. So by the wrists and the ankles they were nailed to the wood and hung up there totally naked. Pictures of the crucifixion usually include a loincloth, but that was not true. They were exposed totally to public humiliation; then they were left there without food or drink.

Crucifixion killed by suffocation—being unable to breathe. While there was still strength in the limbs, a victim could push up with the feet and breathe and then when the pain in the ankles got too much, they would relax and hang by the wrists, but then it was more difficult to breathe. So they would push up again as soon as the pain in the ankles had lessened a wee bit. This constant pushing up and slumping, pushing up and slumping gradually made the body all too weak. There came a moment when the legs could not support the weight and push up. That's when suffocation began and they died because the pressure on their lungs was too great. As mentioned already, it took two to seven days to accomplish the death of a victim while they hung naked for the world to mock and abuse. It was a dreadful death.

No Roman citizen was ever crucified—it was considered too undignified for them. You are already, I hope, asking, "Why, then, did it only take six hours for Jesus to die?" We will have to answer that question. For the moment we just point out what a dreadful death it is.

I want to explain first how Jesus — a good man, as even his enemies acknowledged; one who did nothing but good for people – came to such an end within three short years. We must find a human explanation. The answer is that had Jesus been born at any other time or any other place, it would not have happened; he might have died of old age. But the situation into which he came was such that it was inevitable he would be crucified. Why?

Jesus was, is, and always will be a Jew. He was born into the Jewish people who were living in their own land which had been promised them by God, but they were not their own masters. Since returning from exile in Babylon, they had been under foreign powers continuously. They got their land back, not their freedom and autonomy. They were under the control of others from the day they returned from Babylon. Syria, Egypt, Greece and, finally, Rome conquered them. They only had one very brief period under Greece when a family called the Maccabees rebelled. Bravely, Judas Maccabeus, whom they nicknamed 'The Hammer' hammered the Greeks and gained for the Jews a few precious years during which they had political freedom. However, they soon lost it again and Rome was the most powerful occupying force they had ever known.

God waited until the Jews were under Rome before he sent his Son to the Jewish people. That tells you that it was a necessary situation for him to face. God had waited centuries to send his Son, he had not been speaking to the Jews for three hundred years, but when the fullness of time came, he sent his Son and everything was absolutely right for what

God wanted to achieve through his Son's becoming flesh and living among us.

Rome was a cruel occupying power. For one thing, they taxed the people heavily, through tax collectors. These people were agents for the enemy occupying power; they were able to make huge profits on the taxes they had to collect for Rome, and they put the profits into their own pockets—men like Zacchaeus. But it wasn't just taxes. For example, a Roman soldier could force you to carry all his kit—for one mile (and no further). So in front of your fellow countrymen you were carrying the Roman soldier's baggage—very humiliating, which makes it all the worse. Jesus said, "If anybody forces you to go one mile, go two." That would be about the most unpopular teaching in that situation, as you can imagine.

One other thing the Romans insisted on, which has a bearing on what follows, is that they forbade the Jews to impose capital punishment. Of course in the Mosaic Law there were about fifteen crimes or sins for which God had told them to take the life of the guilty sinner, but now they could not do that. Rome reserved the right of capital punishment to itself and the Jews were no longer allowed to put anyone to death. That was why Jesus had two trials—one before the Jewish leaders and one before Pontius Pilate—he had to. They wanted him to die but they couldn't put him to death legally. They had to get Rome to do it, which, incidentally, tells us that Gentiles are just as responsible for the death of Jesus as Jews. Indeed, Jesus said so. He said, "The Son of Man will be delivered to Gentiles to put to death." Yet for two thousand years the Gentile Church has been blaming the Jews for the death of Jesus. We are all involved—Jew and

Gentile. If the Jews were involved in the death of Jesus, so were we, the Gentiles. So that was the situation into which Jesus was born: a country occupied by a cruel, strong and well-organised enemy.

Now what happens in an occupied country? The USA has never been occupied by an enemy, and Britain hasn't for a long time, though in World War II we came very near it when Hitler was poised to invade. That was a desperate situation largely changed by a few very brave Royal Air Force pilots in the Battle of Britain. But France, Belgium, Holland, Denmark and Norway were among the occupied nations.

What happened in those countries in World War II is exactly what was happening in the Jewish nation under the Romans. The native people divided into three groups, very clearly. First, there were the collaborators — those who gave way and co-operated with the enemy occupiers, making the best of a bad job, selling themselves to the enemy. The collaborators in Jesus' day were called the Sadducees. The High Priests belonged to that group, and they collaborated with the Romans in governing the place.

The second group is those who fight, rebelling against the situation. They are called terrorists by the enemy occupying power. They call themselves 'freedom fighters'. In Jesus' day they called themselves 'Zealots'. Of course, they were hunted down and many were killed. So they had to go and hide in the mountains, particularly the mountains of Galilee, from which they would come out at night and make raiding parties against the Roman troops. Jesus had one Zealot among his twelve disciples, who was called Simon.

The third group is the religious group, and they retreat from the whole mess into their religion; they were represented then by the Pharisees. They were convinced that the people of God were being occupied by an enemy because they were not keeping the Law of Moses, so they retreated from ordinary life into the Law of Moses, and they had Moses' 613 laws and thousands of others. To take one example, they had taken the Sabbath law and made it into a thousand prohibitions on the Sabbath. You may laugh at them but, really, some of them were so ludicrous. You must not drag a stick in the dust if you are using a stick on the Sabbath. If you made a line in the dust with your stick, you were ploughing, and that is forbidden on the Sabbath. They were not allowed to wear false teeth on the Sabbath—that is carrying a burden. They were not allowed to pin their clothes together with a safety pin or a pin because that was sewing.

Do you know they still have these laws? If you get into a lift (elevator) in Jerusalem on the Sabbath, you are not allowed to press the button—that's work. So on the Sabbath they have special Sabbath elevators and they stop at each floor and go on automatically so you don't have to press a button. Or if you can't use the elevator you have to walk up ten flights of stairs; that's not work, but pressing the button is work. The signallers in the Israeli army use Morse code with a Morse key tapping it, but the Chief Rabbi said that you mustn't do that on the Sabbath because it is work. They said, 'But Rabbi, we're fighting on the Sabbath. The enemy doesn't stop fighting; we're going to have to signal on the Sabbath.' He thought for a long time and he said, 'All right then. If you use your left hand on the Sabbath, that's not work. But if you use your right hand. . . .'

You may laugh at these things but it is going on even today. They are still working out in detail how to apply every law of Moses, and that was what the Pharisees were doing. Jesus rode roughshod over their traditions. That got him into trouble with them, but do you realise that Jesus would so easily get into trouble with all those three groups from what he said, from what he did, and from what he allowed his disciples to do. All three groups would come to hate him. In other words, Jesus would get into trouble with someone, and Jesus was his own man but everybody was asking which group he would line up with or join — which would put him out of favour with the other two. But if he didn't join any of them, he would put all three out of place. He would certainly become a very unpopular person.

However, his popularity with the ordinary folk was an added problem. Those three groups already had problems with him, but all three had one big problem and that was that he was so popular that people flocked to him. He was becoming a major figure within months of beginning his public ministry. He was a major threat to anybody trying to lead the country, and it would become worse. He was bound to antagonise someone, to inflame them to anger or envy.

The hostility began before Jesus had done a single thing — from his own village. Only a few months after he began to preach he went to his own village of Nazareth, and they tried to assassinate him. All he had done was read from the scriptures and add a few words. Didn't they like the sermon? No, they didn't, but who throws a preacher off a cliff because they don't like a sermon? They took him from the synagogue to the cliff which you can see today outside Nazareth, where they tried to throw him off the cliff. Was it because they thought he was an egomaniac, because he applied the scripture to himself and virtually said, 'I'm the fulfilment of that Scripture'? That is not why they did it.

I'll tell you why they did it: they were afraid of the Romans, and if someone from Nazareth started making claims to be the Messiah, they knew what the Romans would do. They would come and wipe out Nazareth. They would take vengeance on them. They saw Jesus after only a few months of preaching as a threat to their village. 'Rather him than us — let's get rid of him straightaway.' That was the first of many attempts to assassinate Jesus. The very first had been when he was only a few months old, in Bethlehem. He had done nothing then but they tried to kill him. Now just a few months into his ministry, they were trying to kill him.

When he went south to Jerusalem they had a big public debate about fatherhood. The Jews claimed Abraham as their father, but they said to Jesus, "You don't know who your father is" — a very nasty remark. They had heard that Mary had been pregnant and not by Joseph before her wedding. The rumour had spread — and it is still spreading. Do you know that there was a rumour that Jesus was the result of Mary being raped by a Roman soldier and that actually he was the son of a Roman soldier? That is still going around, and it began in his day. They said, "You don't even know who your father is, but Abraham is our father."

Actually, Abraham was in Jesus' family tree as well but he said, "Abraham, your father? The devil is your father." He said, "I can prove it because he's the father of lies — he doesn't tell the truth, and you are telling lies about me. So you must be his children." Actually, he said, "I do know who my father is, and my father knows all about you." It's a nasty set of arguments. Then when they claimed Abraham as their father, he said, "Abraham — he was thrilled when I came."

They said, "You're not fifty years old. Abraham's been dead two thousand years." He said, "Before Abraham was, I AM." That's God's name: I AM. The Jews immediately took up stones to stone him to death in spite of being forbidden to by the Romans. That was yet another attempt at his life.

In just three years there were several attempts to kill Jesus and he escaped from all of them. Well, you can see how he became an enemy of many people. In fact, it would be true to say that he had as many enemies as he did friends. All this was bound to lead up to a crisis. It was Jesus himself who actually started the crisis. He finally staged an entry into Jerusalem publicly and the crowds turned out to see him because they had all come to Jerusalem for the Feast of Passover and he chose his time carefully. The Mount of Olives was where the men of Galilee pitched their tents, and he was very popular with many of the Galileans. So he chose to ride into Jerusalem on a donkey through the Galilean camp on the Mount of Olives where many would gather.

I can remember one Palm Sunday I had joined in a procession of people from all kinds of churches from Bethany to Jerusalem — crowds still turn out every Palm Sunday to see it, but we were in the middle of the procession and we started singing. The church authorities told us to keep quiet and I felt like saying, 'If we keep quiet, the stones will cry out.' But they put us at the very back of the procession where we danced and sang and a young Roman Catholic priest joined us with a big banner, 'Jesus, What a Wonder You Are.' We sang and danced all the way into Jerusalem. Everybody else in the procession was shuffling along in silence, which seemed to me so odd on Palm Sunday, but the original Palm Sunday procession was not quiet; it was noisy. They told them to be quiet, and that was when Jesus said, "If they're quiet, the stones will cry out and shout out."

He was deliberately staging a public spectacle to challenge the authorities because he had now decided that he was ready to die, and there would be no escape. It is interesting how the crowds welcomed him: they tore palm branches off the trees, threw them on the ground; they took their coats off and threw them on the ground too, even for the donkey to walk on. They were shouting, "Hosanna! Hosanna!" Now we think that's a new chorus—something to sing—but it isn't. 'Hosanna' means 'Liberate us, set us free, now! Freedom now!' It was a demand, and they honestly thought that Jesus was going to come and deal with the Romans at last. None of them noticed that he was riding on a donkey. If you are coming to conquer, you come on a horse. When Jesus comes back the second time, he is coming on a horse but this time he came on a donkey, in peace. They never noticed that he was weeping—over Jerusalem. He was crying but they didn't notice. They had their agenda: freedom now. Liberate us now! Hosanna! So we turn it into a nice, polite greeting but that's what it means.

It was a deliberate challenge to the authorities, Roman and Jewish. But he came up the final slope to the Eastern Gate and went through the gate, and that was when the crowd fell silent because he didn't turn to the right—he turned to the left. Now you don't know the significance of that unless you have been there. On the right was the Roman fortress, the base for their soldiers in Jerusalem—the Fortress Antonia. You can still visit it. On the left was the Jewish temple. Jesus came up into the gate and turned left. That was altogether wrong—a total surprise. The crowd fell silent. Jesus borrowed a whip, and he went into the temple and whipped Jews. That could hardly have been more unpopular a thing to do, and he whipped them out of the temple. Single handed, he cleared the outer courtyard of the temple.

That outer courtyard was worse than a marketplace. It was where you had to change your money because the temple authorities would not accept ordinary money. They would only accept temple coins in the offering. So they had money-changers in the outer courtyard who would change your money for temple money — at a high price. Jesus called them a 'den of thieves'. There were animals and doves in the outer courtyard that were sold for exorbitant prices for sacrifice. The whole thing was turned into a market and a market where you were fleeced of your money very easily.

Jesus was very angry because that outer courtyard was the only part of the temple where Gentiles could come and pray. It was a house of prayer for all nations, and now there was the noise, and the animals, and the money changers were shouting and trying to make money, and doing it very successfully. Jesus went into that courtyard, and in sheer anger whipped not the animals but the men who were selling them. He drove them out of that courtyard by sheer force of personality — but can you imagine what that would do and the effect of it, and the disappointment of the crowd? If you want to know why the crowd was shouting for Jesus' death just a few days later — that is the reason. They pinned their hopes on a conquering king coming in and getting rid of the Romans, and now all he did was whip the Jews — terribly tactless! Jesus was neither tactful nor tolerant. He said, "Zeal for my Father's house has eaten me up." He was very angry, and his sheer anger cleaned the temple up. But what a challenge to the Jewish authorities, and they took up the challenge very quickly. They held a special meeting, and they said, "What can we do about this man? The world is going after him. What is he going to do next? If he isn't careful, he will have the Romans come and just destroy us. It's either him or us; it's either him or the people." They decided he had to go. "If we don't deal with him now, before the Feast comes, we're going to be in real trouble."

They had two problems to overcome. First was the problem: how do you get hold of him? Because every night he was out of the city, and they didn't know where he was staying. Only during the day was he in the city, and then he was surrounded by crowds. They had to find a way of finding him on his own, when they could secretly whisk him away. That problem was soon solved because one of his own twelve followers was too fond of money, and saw a chance to make some for himself. He made a bargain with them for thirty pieces of silver. That was the price of a slave, and to have a slave put you up in the social scale. Judas Iscariot saw his chance. "Thirty pieces and I'll tell you where you can lay hands on him secretly—where he'll be on his own." That chance came as we know in the garden of Gethsemane when for the first time Jesus didn't go to his lodgings outside the city but stayed within the reach of the temple authorities. So that was one problem solved.

The other problem was this: they knew the law and, therefore, if they were going to be accepted by the people, they had to find a crime deserving the penalty of death in the Mosaic Law. Now there are fifteen crimes for which the Mosaic Jewish law advocates the capital punishment penalty. I made a little list of them: fornication, adultery, idolatry, buggery with animals, disobedience to parents—you could have a son killed for that—incest, and so it went on. I can imagine those authorities discussing . . . .

"Well, we don't think he's done any of those."

Then somebody says, "But there's one thing he's done that deserves the death penalty."

"Oh, what's that?"

"Blasphemy."

Anyone who calls himself 'God' is guilty of blasphemy, and blasphemy deserves the death penalty. It does in Muslim law as well.

So now they had got a crime that deserved death. They had got someone who would lead them to him when he was alone after dark. They had everything ready and so he was arrested in the garden of Gethsemane, betrayed by Judas Iscariot with a kiss. What a kiss!

He was put on trial first in a secret trial in darkness, which is illegal. It is still the law that all serious trials must be during the day, but this was night. They were breaking the law. If they could prove that he claimed to be God, then they could claim the death penalty for him, even though they couldn't execute it.

The trouble was that they couldn't find two witnesses to agree on what he had said; they were garbled versions, second-hand versions of what he had said. You have to get at least two or three witnesses for a Jewish law court, who testify to the same words or deeds. They couldn't find them so the judge did an illegal thing. He commanded the prisoner to condemn himself out of his own mouth. He was at perfect liberty to stay silent; you can't make a prisoner condemn himself out of his own mouth—that's not lawful.

But the judge said, "I adjure you by the living God—tell us, are you the Son of God?" Jesus simply said, "I AM." Now that's the name of God. The trial was finished. The judge tore his clothes and said, "You've heard him. You've heard it out of your own mouth. There are seventy of you. You've all witnessed it. We've got the case. What's your verdict?" From every part the assembly heard, "Death, death, death."

There were only two people who didn't vote for his death. One was called Nicodemus, who had met him by night months earlier; the other was called Joseph who came from a place called Arimathea—both of them would play a crucial role later, but sixty-eight people voted for his death, and it was settled. He deserved death in their eyes, guilty of blasphemy. How then to get him killed? They knew that only the Romans would do it so they took him to the Romans.

Now here they ran into another huge problem. In Roman law, blasphemy is not a crime. You can say what you like under Roman law. You can call yourself 'God' under Roman law. They would probably build you a temple and worship you. So what accusation could they bring to the Roman governor Pontius Pilate? That man's name has gone down into history. When you say the Apostles' Creed, you say, 'Suffered under Pontius Pilate'. He has been famous for two thousand years, and yet scholars doubted whether such a man ever existed because no archaeologists uncovered his name until the 1920s when they found a stone in Caesarea, the port on the Mediterranean coast where he had his headquarters. He only went up to Jerusalem for the feasts. In Caesarea they found the stone, 'Pontus Pilatus', and they knew he must be real. It's amazing; they wouldn't accept the word of the Bible for years but they accept a bit of stone. Crazy, isn't it? But that was it.

Pontius Pilate was the worst kind of governor. He had started life as a slave; he was born to a slave family, and he had worked his way up socially. He had become a governor but in many ways he still had a slave mentality. He had already in Israel crucified three thousand people—a very common occurrence. Amazingly, you may never have heard about any other crosses except the one, or maybe the three. But there were thousands of crosses. Anything that happened, he just crucified people. He had stolen money from the temple which people had given for the worship of God, and he took that money to build an aqueduct into the city to bring in more water. That had started a Jewish riot which he had put down by force, crucifying its ringleaders. That's the man before whom they brought Jesus that day for a Roman trial.

The more Pilate talked to Jesus, the more convinced he was that he was totally innocent. But the charge they brought was not, 'This man says he's God—that's blasphemy.' They changed the charge of blasphemy to treason, "This man says he's king, and we have no king but Caesar." Treason was a crime in Roman law which was punishable by death. Can you see how they were manoeuvring, manipulating — from a secret trial in darkness, now it is broad daylight, and it's in public, and now they bring the charge of treason. Pilate tried everything he knew to get out of judging this man. He tried offering to release him. He said, "You know it is the custom for me to release a prisoner to you at Passover. Then I'll do so, but I'll give you the choice," and they hauled a man out of prison called Barabbas. That means, 'son of the father'. The amazing thing is that his first name was 'Jesus'.

What an irony of history. Two people called Jesus, son of the father, and Pilate said, "Which do you want me to release?"

Now Barabbas was a freedom fighter, a terrorist, and the crowds said, "Barabbas! Release Barabbas!" He said, "Well look, if I flog Jesus to within an inch of his life—if I get him whipped—perhaps that'll satisfy you." He sent Jesus away, and they flogged Jesus with the most terrible whip, with long strands of leather, with sharp stones or pieces of bone tied at intervals down those strands of leather. It's a horrible instrument, and it just fillets your flesh to the bone. They flogged Jesus, and they mocked him. They put a crown of thorns on him. They spat on him. They did everything they could to humiliate him until this bleeding, broken body comes back with the soldier. Pilate says, "There. Do you think he looks like a king now? Behold, your king." But they were still after his blood.

Then he got a message from his wife, who said, "I've had a dream. Don't have anything to do with this just man!" This put Pilate in a real fix, and the fix was that already Jews had sent bad reports about Pilate to the Roman emperor at the way he handled his job. The Emperor had said to Pilate, "You mess things up with the Jews once more, and you're out of a job." So Pilate, with his whole career at stake—yet knowing the man is innocent—washed his hands and said, "I wash my hands of this matter. You can do what you like with him," giving them permission to have him crucified. So the trial was over, and Jesus was crucified.

Now a victim had to carry the crossbar of the cross all the way to the crucifixion with his arms tied to that beam. Others carried the long beam. As Jesus carried that beam through the city, people laughed at him and mocked him. Women wept for him, and he turned on them and said, "Women, why are you weeping for me? Weep for yourselves." Then He said a most unusual thing. He said, "If they do these things when the wood is green, what will they do when it is dry?" That is a carpenter speaking — his carpenter mind. As a soldier in front of him is carrying hammer and nails, he is carrying the wood, and he reverts to carpenter's language. You don't cut wood when it is green. You wait until it is dry, matured and ripe, then you start shaping it. He said, "They're doing this to me as green wood. What will they do to you when you are ripe for judgment?" Jesus was seeing that in just forty years ahead when the Jews were ripening for rebellion, Jerusalem would be sacked. "Women of Jerusalem don't weep for me. Weep for yourselves. If they do this to me when the wood is green, what will they do to you when the wood is cured?"

Then Jesus fell. After all, he had not eaten since the Last Supper, he had been flogged to within an inch of his life, and now he was weak. When your arms are tied to a beam like this and you fall, you fall on your face. It's very painful and very damaging. They realised he was weak. So they took the beam off him, and there was an African standing by, Simon of Cyrene. They said, "You must carry this one mile." He took up the cross. Interestingly, we are told that he was the father of two later Christians. I think just carrying the cross for Jesus had done something in him. He became a well-known Christian. It is the most romantic story, and it is true.

Then they got to the place of crucifixion. They took all his clothes off him. I have only ever seen one crucifix where Jesus is not decently covered with a loincloth. It is in Gaudi's Basilica of the Holy Family in Barcelona, Spain—that extraordinary construction. I just noticed when I saw the cathedral there was a life-sized crucifix above the west door, and that Jesus was totally naked. Then they gambled for his clothes. That was the prize, the loot for soldiers who had the distasteful job. Funnily enough, that had been predicted a thousand years earlier in Psalm 22. But they did it because he only wore one superb cloth coat—which women must have made for him—and they didn't tear it into pieces but gambled for the whole thing.

They put the nails through the wrists and the ankles, then dropped the cross into its socket, which caused intense pain. Do you know the word 'excruciating'? It has the word 'cross' in the middle of it, and that's why, because there is no worse pain. He is now in the place where torture begins.

He only lasted six hours, and again I will tell you why shortly. You can divide that time into three hours from nine o'clock in the morning till midday, and then three hours from midday to three. It very neatly divides because, for one thing, it was only from midday to three that the sun went out, and it was all in darkness for three hours.

During the first three hours, his concern was for other people: three in particular. His first concern on the cross was for the feelings of the soldiers who had nailed him. He shouted, "Father, forgive them. They don't know what they are doing." So he was concerned for those who had actually put the nails in, thinking of the day when they would stand before their God to account for their lives. Next he was concerned for the two criminals on two crosses either side of him, one of whom mocked him. But the other said, "You shouldn't be doing that. We deserve this, but he doesn't." That dying thief (perhaps a terrorist, we don't know) saw in Jesus the King of the future and said, "Lord, remember me when you come into your Kingdom." What a statement of faith: to look at this dying, bleeding man and say, "You're a King, and you're going to have a Kingdom; I believe it!" Because above Jesus' head Pilate had had the courage to write the crime for which he was being crucified, 'King of the Jews'. They always put the crime on a notice above their heads as a warning to other people, 'Don't do this.'

Jesus said, "Today, you will be with me in Paradise." Today!

The third person he was concerned about in the first three hours was his mother. She was there. By the way, his earthly mother was at the cross, but his heavenly Father wasn't—as we shall see in a moment. But the sword was piercing Mary's heart now as she saw her son die. I know from experience what it is to have one of your children die before you. You don't expect it; it's not right. Here she is seeing her son die and so he arranged for her to be adopted by the apostle John, who was also there—the only apostle who was. He said, "John, your mother; mother, your son." It says John took her away from the cross from that very moment — so she didn't have to see it.

From twelve till three it's a very different situation because now everything Jesus says is about himself. The first words were, "I'm thirsty," because the body gets dehydrated. As a tease they gave him vinegar to drink, and you know that vinegar doesn't satisfy thirst; it makes it worse. Then there was the loneliness: He realised his Father God was not there, and he said, "My God, my God, why have you left me?" It was a terrible loneliness. It was the first time in all eternity he had ever been on his own without his Father. Then he cried out, "It's finished, it's over." He realised that he was to suffer no more. So at the very last, the fourth thing he said was to use the prayer that his mother Mary had taught him as a little boy. It's from a psalm, and every Jewish boy is taught to say this prayer when they go to bed at night. "Into your hands I commit my spirit." He just added the one word, "Father". "Daddy, into your hands I commit my spirit." He had spoken seven times.

We know why Jesus died in just six hours. The only way to ensure that someone dies quickly on a cross is to break his legs—then he can't push himself up and he can't breathe. They came because it was three o'clock in the afternoon when the Passover began at six, and the Jews told Pilate, "You can't leave dead bodies hanging up there on the Feast of Passover." So the soldiers came, they broke the legs of the two thieves, and then they suffocated. They came to Jesus, and he was dead already. How come? To make absolutely sure, they pushed a spear up under his ribs into his heart, and John, who had come back to the cross after taking Mary away, said, "There was a flow of blood, then water came out of that spear thrust." That is the clue. It's a most unusual thing to happen. A doctor in Ireland made a series of experiments piercing a dead pig's heart to see if he could reduplicate that extraordinary symptom. It could only mean that he did not die of crucifixion. The cross did not kill Jesus.

So what did? The answer is, very simply, a ruptured pericardium. That is the medical term, but in plain English: a broken heart. That is what Jesus died of.

We have been looking at the cross from a human angle. How could a good man come to that end within three years? I hope I have explained it enough for you, but that is not the whole story. We will begin to look at it from God's point of view and say, 'Why did God allow it?' Even Jesus himself was asking God "Why?" at the height of the awful pain and agony of it.

There is no question about it, this death of Jesus was the greatest miscarriage of justice there has ever been, which raises the question: 'Who do we blame? Who was responsible for Jesus dying on a cross?'

Well of course we could say that the Jews were: Pharisees and Sadducees, the high priest Caiaphas, the Sanhedrin. We could say the Romans were responsible, Pilate at the top and the soldiers who actually did the dirty deed. But who caused him to die?

The first surprising answer we must accept is that Jesus caused his own death. He expected to die, he had predicted it many times already but he arranged his death. He arranged *where* he would die. He said, "A prophet must not die outside Jerusalem." He set his face to go to Jerusalem. He decided *when* to die on the day before the Passover feast began. The intriguing thing is that on that day the Passover lamb was killed at three o'clock in the afternoon. At the very moment Jesus breathed his last, hundreds and hundreds of lambs had their throats cut. It is no wonder that Jesus is our Passover lamb. He arranged the timing perfectly and he arranged *how* he should die — on a cross. He had always predicted that he would be crucified and so he had to arrange it. He was in charge of his own death from beginning to end. He said no man takes my life from me, I lay it down. So from one point of view, Jesus' death was suicide, but we can go further than that.

He could have saved himself at any stage in the Garden of Gethsemane. He could have refused to go ahead with it and from then on. When he hung on the cross, he could have ordered the nails out of his hands and feet as easily as we can talk now. That was within his power but he refused, even when they teased him and said, "He saved others, let's see if he can save himself." I am amazed at his remarkable self-control, saying nothing and doing nothing when mocked in that way, but I still haven't got to the root of who was to blame. The key is in the word 'cup'. In the Garden of Gethsemane, when he prayed he said, "Father if it's possible, take this cup from me." Now the word 'cup' used in its literal sense is a drinking vessel, but in its metaphorical sense it is always associated with God's anger—his wrath. If it's not a literal cup then it's the cup of God's anger and that's what Jesus shrank from. He didn't shrink from crucifixion as a physical act—that's not what he was afraid of, that's not what he shrank from. When he prayed in Gethsemane he was under such stress that drops of blood appeared from the pores of his forehead and any doctor will tell you that is a sign of very extreme stress.

Many people went to their deaths on a cross braver than Jesus did, if that was all he was shrinking from. But no, it was something much worse. It was his Father's anger, which he had never known. When you have never known your father angry and suddenly he is angry and you are drinking a cup of his anger, that is a shocking experience. The real truth is that God himself was responsible for Jesus' death. God planned it, God wanted it, and here is a statement from one of Peter's sermons later in the book of Acts: "This man was handed over to you by God's set purpose and foreknowledge." In other words the whole thing had been planned by God himself for his own Son. That was something the world, looking at the cross, did not realise, but it is the truth. It had been planned centuries ago and God sent his Son into the world at just the right time when that would happen.

Now this doesn't mean that we are all puppets in God's hands and that Pilate was predestined to do what he did. I quote Jesus himself on this: "The Son of man must be betrayed." It was inevitable, it was going to happen, but: "Woe to that man by whom he is betrayed." So, in other words, God did not decide *who* would betray Christ but had decided that *someone* would. Woe to the man who chose to be that person, and that was Judas Iscariot and he met a terrible end. He had such regrets about what he had done, betraying Jesus for money, that he went out and hanged himself from a tree overlooking the deepest valley outside Jerusalem, the Valley of Hinnom, and when he threw himself off the cliff, the rope broke and his body fell down and smashed into the ground. We are told his bowels gushed out, and that place is still called, 'The Field of Blood'. Tourists are not taken to see it but I wanted to see it, and someone took me to look down in that deep, horrible valley, so deep that the sun never gets to the bottom. Way down there my guide said, "That's the Field of Blood, that's where Judas finished up." but it was God who ordained that someone would betray his Son. What a choice Judas made, which he almost instantly knew was wrong.

So we can say the death of Jesus was a supernatural event as well as a natural event, a divine event as well as a human event. Earlier, we looked at the human side of the cross, but now I am going to look at the divine side, because there were supernatural events associated with the death of Jesus. Nature, creation, was involved, just as at his birth a star had been his sign. By the way, that does not approve astrology, it is totally different: astrology says the position of stars when a baby was born affects the baby; in Jesus' case, it was the position of the baby that affected the stars, and that is not the same at all. Just as a star heralded Jesus' birth, the sun heralded his death by going out. I don't know exactly what happened but it certainly wasn't an ordinary eclipse, because that only lasts a minute. If you ask me for an explanation, I believe that God piled a very thick cloud above the scene which the sun could not penetrate. For three hours there was darkness, and that is very significant. The Bible talks about the sun being darkened at the end of history but it has happened once already when the wrath of God was poured out on His Son.

There was an earthquake when he died—did you notice that? If you go to the hill called Golgotha, the place of the skull, behind the modern era bus station just outside the city wall on the north, you will see that there are vertical cracks right through the strata, and when you see vertical cracks through the lines of rock going the other way, you know that it is earthquake country. It is all in an earthquake zone and there was an earthquake when Jesus died. The sun went out, darkness came, the earth shook. This was not a natural event but a supernatural event.

Big things were happening. The world of the dead was affected. You read of that in Matthew. You find that cemeteries were shaken, the gravestones were shaken and dead people came out of their graves and were seen walking around. So the death of Jesus was shaking the universe, it was shaking the world of the dead. It was a universal event with universal effect. One of the most extraordinary events was in the temple itself. The veil over the Holy of Holies, where God dwelt in his glory, was a curtain or drape, forty feet high, beautifully embroidered, and that was torn in two from the top to the bottom. That was not a human act; it was God ripping the drape apart. You know one of the signs that a house is empty, is that there are no drapes left. This was God saying, "Look! I've gone; it's empty." God never again sent his glory into that place. All the old sacrificial system in the Holy of Holies and in the holy place was finished when Jesus died, never to be used again because Jesus' sacrifice made every other sacrifice obsolete and of no value.

So it was an extraordinary event, and of course God is light and where God is absent, there is just darkness. He is the source of all natural light as well as his own light of glory and that is why there was such darkness. Yet he was very much involved. To God a thousand years is like a day but it also says, 'A day can be like a thousand years.' I believe that day was like a thousand years to God as he poured his anger on his own Son—it must have seemed endless to God. We often forget the Father's feelings by focusing on the Son's pain, but the Father must have felt it very deeply indeed. Why had he forsaken his Son? And I take it quite literally that he had. Why did he not speak? He spoke at his baptism, he spoke on numerous occasions in Jesus' life and ministry, but now he is totally silent. The truth is that God sent him to earth to die. That was the main purpose for sending him. I almost just want to be silent and let that sink in. What could God accomplish in his death that he couldn't accomplish in his life?

Why is it that the four Gospels in our Bible spend so much time on Jesus' death and so little on his life? A third of the

Gospel stories are about his death. Someone said Mark's Gospel is like an express train slowing up for a station. In the first few pages you are dashing through months and the favourite word is immediately or *straightaway* — and straight away he entered into a boat ... and straight away he was at the other side ... and straight away a man met him outside the tomb.... You are almost breathless in the first few pages of Mark as you dash through two and a half years of ministry. Then it begins to slow down and then you get only months, and then you get only weeks, and then you get every day of the last week and then every hour of the last day. Have you noticed this? There's a deceleration, until you are left looking at the cross as if that has been the point of the whole journey. That is the climax, and Mark, who was obviously a good reporter, a good journalist, has given us this Gospel of the slowing down of time until you stop at the cross. It is an amazing literary device.

Now how do we know why God wanted Jesus to die? There are two qualifying statements about his death made in 1 Corinthians 15, at the beginning of the chapter. Paul says, 'The first important thing about our faith is that Christ *died for our sins according to the Scriptures.*' Those two qualifications are what will help you to understand God's point of view, why he wanted it to happen and why he let it happen to his Son. So I am going to take those two phrases in reverse order. If you want to understand the meaning of the cross, you must first of all see it *according to the scriptures* and the key there is that the scriptures referred to are not your New Testament, which wasn't written when Paul said that. You are to go back to Jesus' Bible and he only had the Old Testament scriptures. So if you want to understand the cross, go to your Old Testament — that is quite a surprise to some people who think that the Old Testament isn't a Christian book and there's no point in Christians reading it!

I was asked to go and speak at a church in England once for a series of five evening meetings during the period they call Lent, which is the period before Easter. The vicar said to me, "David I'd love you to speak about the cross. Could you give me five titles for the talks that I can publicise?" I hate giving titles beforehand because I never know what I am going to speak on but I said, "All right, here are five titles: Genesis, Exodus, Leviticus, Numbers, Deuteronomy." He said, "No, didn't you hear me? I'd like you to talk about the cross." I said, "I'm going to, I'll talk about the cross in Genesis, the cross in Exodus, the cross in Leviticus, the cross in Numbers, and the cross in Deuteronomy." He looked at me as if I was crazy but I gave five evening talks. I wonder if you can guess which part of the books I talked about! In Genesis I talked about Abraham offering Isaac on Mount Moriah when God said, "I'll provide the sacrifice," and provided a lamb to take the place of Isaac—that points straight to the cross! Since Isaac was a full grown man and could have resisted his old father Abraham, it means that Isaac voluntarily submitted, knowing that his father was going to kill him, and said he would go through with it. We had a great evening on the cross from Genesis. In Exodus, I told them about the Passover lamb, and how when the angel of death visited Egypt and took the firstborn of every family and killed them, those who took the blood of the lamb and put it on their doorpost were going to be safe. We, because the blood of Jesus is over us, escape the judgments of God. So I preached on the cross from Exodus. As to the cross from Leviticus — I had to go to chapter 16 where they did an amazing thing. Once a year the high priest would confess the sins of Israel while his hands were on the head of a goat, called the scapegoat, and then they would drive the goat out of the city, out into the wilderness where the goat would die, and hope in this way to get rid of their sins by putting them on the goat and kicking the goat out of the city—what a picture of Jesus.

There is a famous artist called Holman Hunt who painted a picture called 'The Light of the World', in which Jesus is knocking at the door of a human heart. But he painted a picture which to me is much more wonderful called 'The Scapegoat'. He camped by the shores of the Dead Sea to paint it. It was in the days when there were bandits and he had to pray for God to protect him while he did so. It is the picture of an old goat dying by the shores of the Dead Sea, and the look on the goat's face—I just don't know how he has done it—the eyes are like the eyes of Jesus looking at you. He saw the scapegoat as a picture of Jesus being kicked out of the camp and carrying our sins away and dying for us.

Then what about the book of Numbers? It has a most unusual account there of how God fed the people of Israel for forty years. There is no food in the Sinai desert, yet every morning, except on the Sabbath, God sent them food, which lay on the desert floor. God gave them twice as much for the Sabbath on the previous day—a double miracle. They did not know what it was, but it contained all the proteins, minerals and carbohydrates they needed. So they called it, in Hebrew, 'manna', which means 'What is it?' — a good name for it. They had 'What is it' for breakfast, lunch and supper—day in and day out. If you had 'What is it' for as long as that, you would probably do what they did. They began to grumble. They were fed up with a monotonous diet and they thought back to their days in Egypt where even as slaves they had leeks, and garlic, and other foods that stimulated the taste buds. They grumbled and said to Moses, "Go and tell God we're fed up with this 'What is it'." The children used to ask their parents, "What are we going to have for lunch?" "What is it tonight for supper?"

"What is it?"

All were fed up with "What is it?" 'Manna' became almost a dirty word to the Israelites.

Moses went to God and said, "The people are complaining about the food you are providing." They should have been jolly thankful because it meant their survival in the desert but they were fed up. They were grumbling. Typically, we would do the same. God sent snakes among them and many died because the snakes were poisonous, and there were so many snakes that the people began to realise: this is not just a natural phenomenon, God's doing something, he is punishing us for grumbling. And that was right.

So they said to Moses, "Go and ask God and beg him to take the snakes away."

Moses went to God, and God said, "I'm not going to take the snakes away but I will give you a cure for snake bite. Go and make a metal snake and put it up on a pole, and put that pole up on a hill near the camp, and if anybody gets bitten with a snake, all he has to do is climb the hill and gaze on that snake, and the poison will leave." Perfect antidote.

Now that story is in the book of Numbers but it is referred to in John 3:14–15, just before the verse that everybody knows. Nobody seems to know that the snake bites are referred to just before you get to John 3:16 and John 3:16 says, 'And so God loved the world that he gave his only begotten Son.' Or as Jesus himself said a verse or two before, "As Moses lifted up the serpent in the wilderness, even so the Son of Man must be lifted up." That is one of the Old Testament stories that directly show what the cross is about. It is an antidote. God didn't remove the poisonous snakes but he gave them an antidote to cure them of the poison. God still has condemned all of us to death but he has lifted up his Son as an antidote, and if we go and gaze at that Son on the cross, the poison will leave us. There it is.

One of the naughty things I do to prove that we go by text and not context is to ask audiences how many of them can tell me what John 3:16 says. Most can do so. Then I ask, 'How many of you can tell me what John 3:17 says?' Then what John 3:15 says? The thing is that you will never understand John 3:16 if you don't know what John 3:15 and verse 17 say. It is part of an argument on that word "So." It is not that God *so* loved the world, as if so is spelled s-o-o-o-o — and even the Amplified Bible says that God loved the world so much; it is not that at all. The word 'so' there means 'in this way'. *Thus... in this way* God loved the world and gave his only begotten Son. In what way? In the same way that Moses put the serpent up on a pole back in Numbers. You see how the context changes your understanding of a text? I have written a short book entitled *Is John 3:16 the Gospel?* where I have explained it in its context, and it means something quite different than most people think.

Well now the Old Testament scriptures were divided into three parts: the Law—the first five books, the Writings—which included the Psalms, and the Prophets. I have told you about the cross and the Law. Now I will tell you about the cross in the Writings. Psalm 22 is a remarkable psalm. David was writing about things that never happened to him. It is a prophetic psalm, looking at someone else, the Son of David. It begins with these words: 'My God, My God why have you forsaken me?' It goes on to say, 'They have gambled for my clothes,' and, 'They have pierced my hands and my feet.' There are many other things in Psalm 22 which never happened to David, but there is the cross in the Writings.

When we turn to the Prophets, we are almost overwhelmed with references, but I will mention only Isaiah 53. That is the one chapter that is on display in what is called 'The Scroll of the Book' in Jerusalem today, from the Dead Sea Scrolls. They found Isaiah 53 and they put it in a display case, and that chapter talks about someone who was wounded for our transgressions, bruised for our iniquities, the chastisement of our peace was upon him, and by his stripes we are healed. What could be a better description of the cross than that? That never happened to Isaiah but he could see hundreds of years beforehand what God would do, and cause his suffering servant to be punished for the sins of his people. So when we are told he *died according to the scriptures* that means according to the Old Testament. You will find the cross prefigured in every part of the Old Testament, and you will begin to see why Jesus had to die, why God planned it.

Finally, let us look at *He died for our sins*. 'For our sins' — that little phrase completes the understanding and that is what affects each one of us if you put *yourself* into it. He died for your sins. A number of Nazi war criminals were told about this, and one after another they came face-to-face with Jesus and believed in him. *We* were there at the cross. There is a famous song: *Were you there when they crucified my Lord?* — have you heard that song? Dame Myra Hess, who was a famous singer, went to India and gave concerts worldwide and she always sang that song. An Indian leapt to his feet while she sang and said, "Yes! We were all there" — and you were. But I wonder where you would have been. Would you have been among the crowd making fun of Jesus, would you be like the dying thief, would you be like Barabbas? Where would you have been?

Let's think about what it means that Christ died for our sins. I am going to take the word 'cross', C-R-O-S-S, to try and help you understand why God planned the death of his Son. For 'C' we will take the word *conquest*. It was the final victory of Christ over the powers of evil. They were going to do their worst against him and yet still he would not sin. They didn't win the victory, he did. Writing to the Colossians, Paul said, 'Having made a show openly of the principalities and powers, he triumphed over them in his cross.' You see, for Jesus, life had been one long battle, and Satan had tried to make him sin and it failed all the way through.

The cross first, then, is a conquest of the principalities and powers who thought they were winning when they destroyed him, but they were losing. It was the final climactic battle between Jesus and the forces of evil and the evil forces were throwing everything at him in that final battle. But he won, and finished with his trust in God intact. "Father, into your hands I commit my Spirit." The principalities and powers for the first time in history had failed to cause a person to sin—that was the final victory of the cross.

Secondly, the letter 'R' — the cross was a *ransom*. A ransom is paid to deliver someone to freedom who has been kidnapped and the Bible calls Jesus' death a ransom. It doesn't talk about who the ransom was paid to; it is talking about the price that was paid to set people free. For we had all become slaves of sin, kidnapped by Satan, but the cross paid the price and that price was heavy. As I have told you already, every act of forgiveness is written in Jesus' blood. You were redeemed not with silver or gold but with the blood of Jesus Christ. That was the price he paid for your liberation, for bringing you home to God, no longer a slave to sin.

The third letter is 'O' and Christ's death was an *offering*. The Old Testament way of dealing with sin was to compensate God by making an offering to him, usually an innocent animal, and in those days God accepted that death as compensation for the sin that had been committed. It made atonement to God but it never really was adequate because animals cannot make compensation for a human life that has been wrong. Nevertheless, it was that way that God taught them: you could offer atonement to God, a sin offering to God to compensate for your sin. Rather than God taking your life, you offered an innocent life in your place to him and he accepted that until Jesus died, and now he will no longer accept that because that is only an innocent animal and an animal can never compensate for a bad life. Nevertheless, the cross was an offering; it was compensation, an atonement to make up to God for what we had done.

The letter 'S' is *satisfaction*. Justice was satisfied so that mercy could be offered. God is a God of justice. In other words, all sin must be punished if God is righteous. If an innocent man will take the punishment instead of you, that satisfies God's justice. Justice is satisfied and you may go free.

That brings me to the last letter 'S', *substitution*. Quite simply, Jesus died in your place. A missionary friend of mine was preaching about the cross in India again, and an Indian cried out from the congregation, "Away from there Jesus, that is not your place, it is mine!" That man had realised that *he* should have been crucified, not Jesus, and you realise that means that *all of us deserve a premature, violent death*. That would be justice, but because he suffered a premature, violent death, we do not need to.

We can put it this way: when Jesus in the last three hours on the cross was in darkness, was thirsty, was desperately lonely, that is what hell is like. In hell, you are in darkness; in hell you are lonely; in hell you are thirsty—it is a hot place. It means quite simply that in the last three hours on the cross, Jesus went through hell. He experienced hell so that you need never go there. He was your substitute. The first man to realise the truth of substitution at the cross was Barabbas. He was the first man to go free, knowing that Jesus had died as his substitute in his place — that if Jesus had not died, Barabbas would have died.

All of us need to come to the place where we realise that Jesus shouldn't have done that, *we* should. We deserve it, he didn't. He was innocent, we are not. Yet it was he who took our place instead of us on the cross. When you realise that, then something happens inside you but I want to add something very important. The cross was a *double* substitution. Most people only see it as a single substitution. What do I mean? I mean that most people are happy to put their sins onto Jesus. But, 'Him who knew no sin was made sin on our behalf that we might become the righteousness of God in Him.' The double substitution is Jesus saying,

'Give me your sins and I will give you my righteousness', but so many people want to get rid of their sins but are not so happy about *receiving the righteousness*. That is the double substitution and Christ says: For the way you live, I pay and I'm your substitute, but I now want to live in your life and be your substitute in life as well as in death. I want you to be righteous. Give me your sins and I give you my righteousness.

That is double substitution and that is the *whole* gospel. People love the first bit of it and they are not so happy about the next. It is all part of the amazing truth of the cross. We make the cross our own when we are baptised in water. Paul speaks of all of us ... who were ... *baptised into his death*. I will never forget the day I was baptised in a little church up in the hills in the north of England. I was the only person being baptised and they had opened up the pool. It was covered in green slime—it hadn't been open in a long time. I went down thinking I was going to make an interesting study in pond life, but as I went down into that slimy green pool, the pool vanished and I saw Jesus in the muddy Jordan River just being baptised in front of me. It was what we call a vision. I will never forget it. I thought, 'I am just following Jesus down into this slime pool as he went down into the muddy Jordan River for me.'

He didn't need to have sins washed away but he did it for me as he died for me. He began his ministry as a substitute, baptised for me. When we are baptised, we are baptised into his death. It is not enough to say 'Christ died for me.' We need to be able to say 'I died with him.' It is not enough to say 'Christ was buried for me.' We need to be able to say 'I have been buried with him.' It is not enough to say 'Christ rose for me.' We need to say: 'In Christ I have risen with him.' When you were baptised, you were identified with the cross and with his burial and with his resurrection. Who says baptism isn't important? It is the time we get fully identified with Christ and wash away the past and come out of the water to live a new life.

No wonder he told us that is how we begin the Christian life and then we continue it by having the Lord's Supper. You never are allowed to forget the cross and therefore Jesus said, "Whenever you eat...." Actually, he said, "Take some bread, take some wine, and remember that my body was broken for you and my blood was poured out for you." We must live under the cross for the rest of our lives and never forget it. We are crucified with Christ, you were at the cross and you weren't among the crowds mocking him. You weren't one of the thieves. You were on the cross with Jesus and you have been crucified too. The old life is dead and it has gone. You are free now, and he is now your substitute in life as he was in death.

We conclude this chapter by running through the different reactions among people to his death that I have found. Firstly, a very common attitude to his death is *indifference*—'Couldn't care less, doesn't affect me in the slightest.' That is a very difficult attitude to deal with, when they don't seem to feel anything. Indifference is a real problem. After all, it happened so long ago and so far away, why should I be concerned now? In World War I, there was a chaplain to the forces called Studdert Kennedy, known as 'Woodbine Willie' because he gave Woodbine cigarettes to everybody. He wrote a most marvellous poem called *Indifference*, and it really brings the point home, that people would simply pass by:

> When Jesus came to Golgotha, they hanged Him on a tree,
> They drove great nails through hands and feet, and made a Calvary;
> They crowned Him with a crown of thorns,
> red were His wounds and deep,
> For those were crude and cruel days, and human flesh was cheap.

> When Jesus came to Birmingham they simply passed Him by,
> They never hurt a hair of Him, they only let Him die;
> For men had grown more tender, and they would not give Him pain,
> They only just passed down the street, and left Him in the rain.
> Still Jesus cried, "Forgive them, for they know not what they do,"
> And still it rained the wintry rain that drenched Him through and through;

> The crowds went home, and left the streets without a soul to see,
> And Jesus crouched against a wall and cried for Calvary.[1]

Next, there are those who are *interested*—they hear about the cross and they would like to know a little more. There are so many parallel situations today in the world that we can quickly link their thoughts to something almost that has just happened in the world, because 'crucifixion' is happening. Unjust executions, innocence dying—it's happening all the time, all around us, and we can link those innocent deaths and those miscarriages of justice with the death of Jesus and get them more interested.

Then I meet a few people who are *indignant*. They are angry on behalf of Jesus. They say it was wrong that he should be put to death, and all of us get angry about someone innocent who's put to death. It seems such an injustice to us when it happens. People use that as an argument against capital punishment—that sometimes the wrong person is put to death and the innocent person suffers. So there are those who are indignant but still they are thinking about others, not about themselves.

Finally, there are those who are *involved* and who have realised that this event two thousand years ago and thousands of miles away involves them personally and that they were there; that they were part of this sin-sick, sad old world that put Jesus to death. Once you feel yourself identified with the cross of Christ, then life begins to take on a very new purpose and significance. That is why I have been addressing the subject of the cross here — that you may feel involved. It was for you that it happened. When you believe that, you find yourself crucified with Christ; dead to the world and alive to Christ. A whole world has changed for you, and you too are living a new life.

Note
[1] From *The Unutterable Beauty*, the collected poetry of the Revd G.A. Studdert Kennedy, Hodder & Stoughton, 1927.

3

The wonder of his
BURIAL

Let us return to the familiar first three verses of 1 Corinthians 15: 'Now brothers, I want to remind you of the gospel I preached to you which you received and on which you have taken your stand. By this gospel you are saved if you hold firmly to the word I preached to you. Otherwise, you have believed in vain.' Notice that one of the fundamental facts of the gospel to which we are to cling, and by which we are saved, is that in between his death and resurrection Jesus was *buried*. Very few Christians think about the burial of Jesus as a fact of faith — and it is a fact of faith. We are saying, 'I believe that he was buried.' It seems a bit strange though, doesn't it? How does that affect our faith? What if he hadn't been buried? Would that really do something bad to our faith?

Well the fact is that Jesus very nearly wasn't buried. In fact, anybody who was crucified in those days was not buried—that was to bestow a post-mortem dignity on the corpse. It is right and dignified to bury someone who has died, and just to throw the body away is to treat them with contempt, and that was what happened to everyone who was crucified in those days. Their body was thrown away on the city garbage dump. On the south side of Jerusalem is a valley so deep that the sun doesn't get to the bottom of it, and it was used as the city of Jerusalem's garbage dump. The gate on the south side of the old city is still called the 'Dung Gate' because they took all the sewage out and took it over into that deep Valley of Hinnom (in Hebrew, *Gehenna*). When Jesus wanted a picture of hell which would be meaningful to those he was teaching, he called it *Gehenna*, which they knew as a place where they threw their garbage. Everything that was useless to them was thrown away into that valley. So hell is God's garbage dump and it is there that he disposes of useless human beings. When you have something and it has perished, you throw it away – maybe an old car tyre or something like that – because it is no use to you anymore. The Bible says that God *throws* into hell — and that is what you do with garbage, you throw it. You don't place it.

When I first went to Jerusalem, in 1960, the Valley of Hinnom was still the garbage dump and there was blue smoke rising from it. I decided to go down there to see what it was really like, and it smelt of sulphur, bad ashes, brimstone. I could see the rotting remains of food and all the rubbish that had been thrown out of the city. Now you won't see it like that. They have landscaped it and it has become lover's lane where young Israelis go to do their courting in the beautiful garden. There is even an open air theatre where I have preached. I remember saying when I preached there, "This is the first time I've preached in hell and I don't want to do it again," and I have never been back. But that was the Valley of Hinnom, and that was the valley with its cliff sides where Judas tried to hang himself from a tree, the rope broke and his body fell and his bowels gushed out at the bottom, and that is where his body lay among all the stinking rubbish. That was where they used to dump the corpses of anyone who had been crucified and Jesus' body would have joined Judas' body in what's still called *Akeldama*, the Field of Blood. But when the Jewish Council, the Sanhedrin of seventy Jewish leaders, condemned Jesus to death there were two men in that body who abstained from voting and they are called 'secret believers in Jesus'. One was Nicodemus, the man who came to Jesus by night some months earlier, and the other was called Joseph of Arimathea, a wealthy man who had a garden just outside the city walls. That garden backed up against a cliff and in that cliff he had hollowed out a magnificent tomb for himself. He and Nicodemus took the body of Jesus and anointed it with seventy pounds of spices.

This is how they did it. A dead body was wrapped in two pieces of linen. One was a very long strip, some yards long, and that was wrapped around the body from the feet up to the chest. Then they took a smaller strip of linen and wrapped it around the head from the forehead up. As they wrapped the cloth around the body, they sprinkled in the spices — whether to delay the corruption or to overcome the smell of corruption, I don't know, probably a bit of both. So you can imagine a corpse wrapped up but with the face and the shoulders left bare. That is why we will find later, when we think about the resurrection, that the clothes were still in place but had collapsed with no body in them, and the turban was wrapped in a place by itself. All these details are so vivid because they are from eye-witnesses who saw it all.

That deep, dark valley was a horrid place in history. During the time of evil king Manasseh, it was a place of worshipping a pagan god, Molech. Manasseh, the Jewish king, was caught up in that pagan cult and one of their detestable practices was to kill babies as sacrifices to Molech. Manasseh killed his own baby son down in that valley as a sacrifice to Molech.

Jeremiah was involved in that valley at one stage. He was told by God, "Go and look at the potter in Hinnom." Jeremiah went to the potter's house, which stood on the edge of the ravine, and saw him dealing with clay on his wheel. He took a lump of clay, threw it on the wheel and tried to make it into a beautiful, delicate vase. The clay wouldn't run in his hands and so it didn't work out according to what he wanted to do. Maybe the clay was not wet enough or was of the wrong consistency. So he took the clay, made it into a lump and threw it on the wheel again, then made it into a crude, thick kitchen pot instead of a beautiful vase. So it became just a utensil which was almost ugly. Then he took it off the wheel and God said to Jeremiah, "Jeremiah did you notice the lesson of the potter? Who was responsible for the shape that the clay became?"

Now we sing songs like 'You are the potter, we are the clay', as though it was the potter's decision, but it wasn't. It was the clay that was deciding what kind of utensil it became. That is the lesson. We are not just clay to God and he doesn't just make us what he wants us to be. If we have run in his hands, if we are the right kind of clay, he will make us into beautiful people. If we don't allow him to make us what he wants us to be, he will make us ugly people. He wants to create—read this in Jeremiah 18—he wants to create beautiful people, beautiful vases that will hold his mercy. But if they won't become what he wants them to be, he makes them into crude pots, full of his justice. One way or another, the Potter will use you, but it is your decision whether he uses you as a beautiful vase full of his mercy or an ugly pot full of his judgment.

The next day Jeremiah was told to go back to the potter's house. This time the crude pot was so hard and brittle that it could not be moulded into anything else. The sun had dried it out. The potter actually took it and broke it to pieces and threw them into the Valley of Hinnom. That is a picture of what God will do to human beings. He will make them into a beautiful vase, full of his mercy if they will let him, but if they won't run in his hands and won't let the Potter's hands make them that, he will make them into a crude vessel of his judgment. Then they will live to become too hard, it is too late to change them, and they are thrown into Hinnom, into hell. Hell is God's garbage dump for useless people whom he cannot use now for anything. That, to me, is the horror of hell: people who have perished, who are no longer useful for the purpose which God made them, and hell is where they are thrown by God — and to think that Jesus came to help us to avoid that dreadful fate.

That is Hinnom, the valley where they threw the corpses of crucified victims, in among all the rubbish. When I went down into that valley, there was the stink, the smoke and the maggots eating up the old food, and it was the most dreadful place you could imagine. I am just sorry that they didn't leave it like that so that tourists could see, but they were never taken there although it is only a few hundred yards outside the city of Jerusalem. If you have been to Israel, they will not have taken you to see it, and they would not have told you about it because it is not a very nice part of Israel's history.

So Jesus very nearly wasn't buried, but Joseph of Arimathea who had that tomb carved out of the rock said,

"He can have my tomb." He was almost trying to make up for the fact that he had only abstained from voting when Jesus was condemned to death. So he and Nicodemus carried the body. There was some kind of funeral. They carried the body from the cross, having obtained permission to do so, and then they wrapped it in the linen cloths with the spices in between, and they laid the body in his tomb. Then they rolled a great stone across the entrance. That stone probably weighed between two and three tons. According to one early manuscript of the Gospel, twenty men were needed to roll it into place. They wanted to make sure that he was in there and stayed in there. So Jesus was buried in that tomb.

Six hundred years earlier, Isaiah had said about the suffering Servant who would die for the sins of the people, that they would make his grave with the wicked and with the rich in his death. A puzzling phrase to be in the middle of that prophecy, but he would have made his grave with the wicked in Hinnom, but he did make his grave with the rich in his death, and Jesus was buried in a superb tomb. I am still eighty percent convinced that the garden tomb is that tomb, but I cannot be absolutely dogmatic about that.

The Church of the Holy Sepulchre also claims to be built over the tomb of Jesus. But when you see what is called the garden tomb, everything fits. It was a military man, a Christian, staying in a house on the northern wall of Jerusalem, who looked out in the morning and saw a hill opposite that looked like a gigantic skull with eye sockets and nose socket and a grey mouth. He thought, "That looks like Golgotha." It was called the 'Place of the Skull'. He said, "If it is somewhere near, it would be a tomb." He got some soldiers to help him to dig through sixteen feet of rubbish, and they found the entrance to the tomb, which is now a most beautiful place. If it is not the real location, it feels like the real place. It is a beautiful garden there and you can go into the tomb. The interesting thing is that it was obviously a family tomb, with two long stone beds on either side and a shorter bed at the end. The longer bed on the left-hand side has been horridly chipped out to make it longer. It's a very crude bit of chipping at the foot end as if it was originally carved for a certain length of a person and then had to be used in a hurry for a taller person. Again that seems to point to a very horrid funeral because it was quickly and badly done. But there we are, where it is doesn't really matter. He has risen, and that is what matters. People who have been to the garden tomb have found it a moving experience.

What does all this mean? He had a funeral. Normally the body would have been washed. There was no time for that, but it was wrapped up by those two men. Actually, some weeks earlier, a lady who was a very devoted friend of Jesus, had broken a bottle of precious perfume and poured it all out on him, and he had said, "Don't criticise her." That was because Judas Iscariot had said, "That money would have helped our funds and she has just wasted it." Jesus said, "She hasn't. She has anointed me beforehand for my burial." She has been remembered for that ever since. Somehow she guessed that he would not get a proper funeral. Maybe it was because she had sat at his feet and listened to Jesus, and he may have told her what was going to happen to him. She knew he would not get a decent burial and she had done it anyway as an act of love for him. That had been in Bethany some weeks earlier, and when the women finally came to the tomb on Easter Sunday, they found it was too late. They had brought more spices, more things to look after the body, but there was no body.

The burial of Jesus is vital to our faith. The authorities were not satisfied with a three ton stone over the entrance. They were worried. He had predicted that after three days he would be alive again, when he had also predicted, "I will be delivered to the Gentiles and crucified." He actually knew he would be mocked first. He had told his disciples this but he said, "After three days, I'll be back with you," and they knew that. So the Jews went to the Roman authorities and said, "Will you please put a guard against the tomb." They weren't worried that he would rise from the dead, they didn't believe it. What they were worried about was whether the disciples would break into the tomb, steal the body, and then pretend he was alive again, which could have caused more trouble. So not only was he put in a tomb which was then sealed with a big stone, armed soldiers were there for three whole days after he was put in, so it looked pretty final.

Indeed the first thing we can say about the burial is that it meant that Jesus was really dead. Had there been even a hint of life as they carried the body and anointed it and wrapped it and put it in the tomb, they would have rushed him off and tried to recover his life — but he was really dead. When you have handled a dead body and done all that, you know that the person is dead, and already *rigor mortis* is setting in. So the fact that he was buried, and that his body was handled when it was cold and dead, means that there was no sign of life whatever.

Then to put him in the tomb, and rolling a stone to stop him from ever getting out, means that they were convinced he was beyond hope. It is important that he really was dead.

Even today people come up with theories that he had only swooned on the cross. He had been flogged to within an inch of his life, he had had no meal since the Last Supper and he had been badly treated, nailed to the wood, a spear in his side, and still people today say he really didn't die, he only swooned, and he recovered in the cool of the tomb. It is amazing how desperate people are to try to prove that the account is not true.

The second thing about a burial is that it is final. As a pastor, I have had many occasions when a husband had died and I would go to visit the widow in the home and she would always talk about her husband in the present tense. She would say, "My husband is in the front room, would you like to see him?" I would go with her into the front room and there he lay, laid out. She would stroke his hair and make the pillow more comfortable for him as if he was just asleep, and she would use that present tense, "He is in the front room," not his *body* is but *he* is. But I noticed that when we had the funeral and we took the husband's body away and buried it, and so she would never see it again, she then changed the tense of her conversation to the past tense. We usually have a meal after a funeral in England, and as we had the meal she would say, "My husband was a very good man, my husband was a good husband to me and a good father to the children." She has changed from saying, 'He *is*' to 'He *was*'. The thing that has changed that is not his death but his burial. The burial somehow becomes the final goodbye. As long as you can still see the body, you have this illusion that in a sense he is still with you, but once the body has been put out of sight, never to be seen again, you accept that is final. That's the end. I have even known widows who tried to raise their husbands from the dead while his body was still with them, but they never try after he is buried. That settles it. Not only is a person really dead, but he is dead and buried, settled, finished, nobody will ever see him again—that's the end of that man. That is what the burial means, humanly speaking. That should have been the end of the story of Jesus but, as we know, it wasn't.

The burial also meant that he was beyond the reach of people to do anything, even with the body. He could not be reached. Man could do nothing more for Jesus from that point of his burial: finished, over, beyond reach. There is only one person who could do anything for him now, and that is God himself. Just as in the darkness of the womb at the beginning, God created a male sperm that fertilised Mary's egg and produced the human Jesus, now God, in the darkness of the tomb, was going to do an amazing miracle. He did both out of the sight of people and beyond the reach of people, but he was going to do another miracle of creation. In the next chapter I will point out to you that the Bible doesn't say 'Jesus rose from the dead', it says God raised him from the dead. He was beyond the reach of man. Only God could do anything inside that tomb, because only God could get into it, and he did that amazing miracle. By the time the tomb was opened again, it would be too late.

Now let us consider a most important question: 'For how long was Jesus buried?' Now it may sound a simple question to you but the trouble is there are contradictory answers in the scripture. One says Jesus himself said he would be three days and three nights in the tomb. You cannot possibly fit that in between Friday afternoon and Sunday morning. Have you been troubled by that? Have you wondered how that can possibly fit? Jesus himself said it: just as Jonah was in the belly of the whale three days and three nights, even so the Son of Man will be in the heart of the earth — but that is impossible: Friday to Sunday. Then if he was three days and three nights in the tomb, how could he rise on the third day? Yet you find that statement in the Gospels: on the third day he rose again—or was raised. This seems a real contradiction and it can be resolved and I want to resolve it for you because I believe every contradiction in scripture can be resolved by knowing further truth.

There were two keys to resolving these contradictions: one is that Hebrew time and Roman time were different. The Hebrews counted a day from sunset to sunset, six p.m. to six p.m., and therefore their whole day consisted of night and day. That is not how we think because we have followed the Roman system of time, from midnight to midnight, and we talk about a whole day as a day and a night, whereas the Hebrews say a night and a day. The Hebrews base their time on Genesis 1 and you notice there was evening and morning the first day, and the earth started in darkness and then became light. So the Hebrews thought God's way, and sunset, six p.m., began the twelve hours of darkness, and the darkness was followed by the light—twelve hours of day. Night and day, evening and morning, darkness and light whereas we think just the opposite. We think of a day as a day followed by the night, the light followed by the darkness. So by Hebrew reckoning he was three days and three nights in the tomb. By Roman reckoning, he was raised on the third day, and that is how that contradiction is resolved. The other key that we need to know is this: Jesus did not die on a Friday—and suddenly the whole thing is released. He died on a Wednesday afternoon at three o'clock. Where then did the Church get such a strong tradition that he died on a Friday, so that they called it 'God's Friday', which later became Good Friday, and good Catholics don't eat meat on a Friday and only eat fish? Where did they get that idea? Well, follow me carefully: Jesus died at three o'clock and they had to get him buried by six o'clock, because six o'clock began the Sabbath. Therefore people said, "Well, if six o'clock began the Sabbath that must have been Saturday, so he died on Friday afternoon." Somehow that's got hold of every Christian and they think that way, but in fact if you read John 19:31 you will find that it says, "Now that Sabbath was a special Sabbath". It was what they called a high Sabbath. It wasn't Friday, and a high Sabbath began the Passover. The Passover began with a special Sabbath where nobody did any work, and that Sabbath could be any day of the week. One other little bit of information which will get you thinking is that Jesus wasn't born in the year zero. Whoever thought our calendar up made a mistake. He was born four years earlier in 4 BC, four years 'before Christ', Christ was born. Unfortunately that mistake has lingered into our calendar. How do we know this? Because when he was born, Herod was still alive, so we know he was born earlier. We know that he died at thirty-three. Now if you add thirty-three to 4 BC, you come to AD 29. In AD 29 the Passover Sabbath was on Thursday—we know that. If Jesus died in AD 29, as everything seems to point to, then Passover began on a Thursday, and the Wednesday was when they killed the Passover lamb, at three o'clock in the afternoon.

So now it all fits beautifully together. Jesus died on Wednesday afternoon at three o'clock. He was crucified at 9 a.m., died by 3 p.m., and was buried by sunset. Then the first day of Passover began with a special Sabbath (see John 19:31). Then there was night (one day, one night); (day two, night three); day (day three), and Hebrew-wise he was – exactly as he said – three days and three nights in the tomb. Notice that he could rise any time after 6 p.m. on Saturday because that is when the first day of the week began for the Jew. It did not begin then for the Roman, but it began for the Jew. So again, everything points to him rising again between 6 p.m. and midnight on the Saturday.

If he rose then, he rose on the first day of the week according to the Jew, but on the third day after he died according to the Roman. Once again we begin to see a reconciling of all the different references. If he died on Wednesday at three and rose again between 6 p.m. and midnight on Saturday, everything fits like a glove. But somehow we think he only rose again in time for Sunday morning at ten (when we worship), but when the women came to the tomb before sunrise it was already empty, having been empty for some hours. Do you see how it all fits together? Now quite frankly it doesn't affect your salvation at all on what day he died, but it does affect your salvation on what day he rose again as we shall see later. So you can dismiss my theory if you like, but to me it is important, when we come across something in scripture and it doesn't fit, that we think it through until it does fit. It is quite exciting when we find that it does.

We have answered the question 'How long was he in the tomb?' but there is a far more important question than that to be asked. That question is the fundamental one about his burial, and it is this: His body was in the tomb but where was *he*? That is a very important question because what death does for us is to separate our body from our spirit, and our spirit goes on. 'John Brown's body lies a-mouldering in his grave, but his soul goes marching on.' Now that is what happens at death. You leave your body behind and your spirit goes on — but where does it go to? And where did Jesus go to? Where was he himself? He left his body in the tomb wrapped up, but where was he?

We have the answer in the Bible — the plain, simple answer, and you wouldn't believe how many Christians don't believe it, and how they argue theologically about it and produce different doctrines. I have to say that later versions of the Apostles' Creed got it wrong with the rendering: 'He suffered under Pontius Pilate, was crucified, dead and buried. He descended into hell.' But the earlier Roman Creed from which it came did not mention 'hell'. The present-day version now renders the text at this point as: 'he descended to the dead'.

All the churches of the East believe he went to hell and that he opened the doors of hell and let everybody out. It is called the 'Harrowing of Hell'. They teach it to all their people but it is not taught in the Western Church at all. Even so, it was believed in the Middle Ages that he went to hell. I am afraid that has appeared again, in the teaching of some of the 'faith' people on television — that he descended into hell after he died and made atonement in hell for us. But I have tried to teach you that Jesus was in hell for the last three hours of his life on the cross. That is when he went to hell. That is when he tasted hell for us, in the darkness when he was thirsty and lonely and without God. Jesus descended into hell spiritually before he died, not afterwards. What the Apostles' Creed should have said but didn't was that he descended into Hades. Unfortunately, most people think they are the same place. Hades is the Greek word for the world of departed spirits and that's all it is. It's not a bad place, nor a good place; it's just where dead people go—where their spirits go when they leave their body behind. The old Hebrew word for Hades was *Sheol* which, again, was simply the world of departed spirits—people who had already died. Their spirits were in *Sheol*, their bodies left in the grave.

Have you noticed in the book of Jonah a very important point: Jonah was dead inside the whale, not alive. Read the book of Jonah carefully and you will find that when the sailors threw him overboard to stop the storm that God had sent, his body sank to the bottom of the Mediterranean Sea. He said, "I lay among the seaweed at the roots of the mountains." Now it takes a minute and a half to drown and it takes more than a minute and a half to go to the bottom of the sea. He said, "The waters engulfed my throat." He describes drowning. So where did he pray from? His body was inside the whale but it says, "He prayed from *Sheol*." His spirit was in *Sheol*.

He said, "I went down to the place where the bars of life closed on me," and he cried — literally, it says so: "I'm crying from *Sheol*." He was dead inside the whale and therefore the whale had picked up a dead body and the whale vomited that body out into the dry land, and that was literally a resurrection from the dead. Do you understand the story now? The whale didn't swallow a live body and he wasn't praying from the whale. He was praying from *Sheol*—his spirit and body separate. That is why Jesus said, "As Jonah was inside the whale, so will the Son of Man be in the heart of the earth." His body would be there but his spirit would be in *Sheol* among those who had already died.

To whom do we owe this information? The answer is Peter. In the First Letter of Peter it tells us exactly where Jesus was and what he was doing. In fact what he says is that Jesus was put to death in the body but alive in the spirit; he then went to *Sheol* and joined the dead people and preached to them. What an amazing bit of information Peter gives us! We know the Lord appeared in the resurrection especially to Peter but we have no record of where it was, when it was, or what they said to each other. So I have to use my imagination. When Jesus appeared to Peter by himself, Peter would say, "Where on earth have you been?" Jesus would say, "I haven't been on earth, I've been in Hades." "So what in Hades have you been doing?" Jesus told Peter, and Peter has recorded it in his letter—he was preaching the gospel to the dead, but not to all of them. Peter said, 'He only preached it to those who died in Noah's flood.' Noah's flood was two thousand years earlier. What it tells us is that not only was Jesus fully conscious after death, but the people who died in Noah's flood were also fully conscious and able to listen to him fully as he preached.

Now there's a real thought for you. You don't cease to be yourself when you die. Two minutes after you are dead you will be fully conscious and you will know who you are, you will know where you are, you will know who you are with. The proof of it is here: Jesus, between his death and resurrection, went to the world of the dead and preached to those who drowned in the days of Noah and gave them the gospel. I was puzzled about this. I don't have the answer for this from scripture and you can reject it if you will, but

I thought, 'Why would Jesus preach to them—to those who drowned in Noah's flood and only to them?' I came up with this answer: they were the only ones who could complain about the injustice of God by saying, 'You wiped us out before our time.' God had vowed never to do that again and he would never do it again to any generation. So they could have grumbled about the injustice of God of denying them the chance that other generations would get. If that is so then perhaps the Father said to the Son, 'Go and preach to that generation because I wasn't really fair on them, or rather I've been less than fair ever since in not doing it again, but go and preach to them.' Whether that is the right answer or not I don't know. But the fact is that in 1 Peter 3 we read, 'In his spirit he went to the world of the dead and preached to those who had been drowned in the days of Noah.' What an amazing fact to reveal. The problem is that when most churches have what they call 'Holy Week Services' they go right through from Sunday to Friday and then they don't meet again till Sunday. There are no Saturday Holy Week services. Therefore, few have been told what Jesus was doing on the Saturday—we just overlook that. Maybe this is the first time you have ever heard this. Well, I beg you, check me out. Don't believe anything David Pawson says—I know him too well. Don't you be fooled, go and check in your Bible. Read your Bible and see whether what I'm telling you is God's Word. If you can't find it in your Bible, forget it. For God's sake forget it and don't go away having roast preacher for your next meal!

So what Jesus was doing between his death and resurrection was preaching to the dead, and you will find in 1 Peter 4 again a reference that the gospel was preached to the dead. Then he came back to life here.

Now while you are separated from your body, you really can have no normal contact with people still on earth. That is what makes death such a bereavement to us. We know as soon as a loved one dies, we cannot talk to them and have them. We are cut off from them because death may cut you off from the living but it doesn't cut you off from the dead. It is very important to realise this. Let me try and sum this up for you.

There are three phases of human existence which we call *embodied, disembodied, re-embodied* — and every one of us is going to go through these three phases. If you listen to a live talk by me as I deliver it, then you are in the embodied phase now, and I can only communicate with you because I also am embodied, but one of these days you will find out that I have been disembodied and I will be cut off from you, even though you would be able to hear my recordings and read my books! When my daughter died at thirty-six, I was cut off from her but she's very much alive. She's that sort of girl, a real tomboy, very alive. I'm sure she's even more alive now than she was then, but I cannot communicate.

People try to through spiritualist mediums and it's fatal because demons have a marvellous gift of mimicking people and they can mimic dead people so skilfully that people are fooled. Just occasionally God can allow us to communicate with someone who is dead but it is not an experience to be sought. We are told not to go to mediums, not to go to spirits. Saul did, and Samuel was brought back from the dead to speak to him. Jesus spoke to Moses and Elijah on Mount Hermon. So there are occasional communications between the dead and the living in the Bible but only when

God ordains it—we are not to seek it. I am looking forward to being with my daughter again and communicating with her again, but I know who she is with and I'm afraid I have asked a number of dying people to give my love to my daughter. Does that sound strange to you? But they will meet her before I do. So I wanted to pass on a message. Actually I have found that really gives them hope because they realise I really do believe in life after death.

So we are in this embodied stage, and the body is really quite a limitation to us. The spirit is set free at death and will be with Jesus and with his people in full communication, in full awareness and consciousness but cut off from us temporarily. The third phase of human existence is to have a new body and become re-embodied, not a reincarnation. I don't believe in reincarnation, because the reincarnation theory is that you come back as someone else and even an animal if you haven't been very good. There's an old song about, 'Be careful because a duck could be somebody's mother.' Do you remember that song? But that's reincarnation and it is rubbish—don't believe in that, but you will be re-embodied as yourself in your own body and that is wonderful news. Therefore we go through these three 'rooms' — from phase one to phase two, from embodied to disembodied, one by one. But we shall go through from room two to room three to be re-embodied together, or rather there will be two days, two different days, on which the righteous are re-embodied and the wicked are re-embodied later. It is where we spend eternity with those bodies that makes all the difference.

Now what I'm going to say is this: Jesus went through all three phases in the space of a week. That this was quicker than anybody else is evident, but he was embodied, he was disembodied and even in that state could go on preaching and teaching, not to the living but to the dead, and then he was re-embodied and that enabled him to communicate with people in this world again. So you see the pattern, and he is called in scripture, our 'Pioneer'. He has gone ahead of us; he is the trailblazer. He has shown us the three stages of all our existence and this embodied phase is simply a preparation for the next two. What we do in this embodied stage is going to affect our entire future, one way or the other, but everybody is going to be raised from the dead, regardless.

What happens to them when they are re-embodied, where they spend that third phase, is the crucial question: it is either a new earth or hell. So if you just think our future is going to happen when we die, that is not the whole future. You are going to come back from heaven anyway to earth. I have conducted funerals for my daughter, for my sister and her husband, and for my mother-in-law at ninety-eight years of age. At each funeral I have said, "They'll be back—one day they will be re-embodied and stand again." You know, looking at the congregation each time, they looked as though I was preaching Buddhism—they had never heard this; they had never seen it in their Bibles but it is there.

So, to summarise, that is what the burial of Jesus is all about. It proves he was dead. He was cut off from us; he was cut off from all his disciples, but he was not cut off from God. He was not cut off from the dead and he went on preaching to them when he couldn't preach to people on earth. That gives you immediately a picture of what will happen to us. We shall be fully conscious immediately after death. We shall be with those who have died already, and especially with Christ and those who have died in Christ. I look forward to that. So if I go before my wife, I say goodbye to her but I say hello to my daughter. It is as real as that and I thank the Lord for being my Pioneer; my trailblazer going ahead and preparing the way, and within one week, assuring me of my future in him.

4

The wonder of his
RESURRECTION

There are plenty of different beliefs about life after death, so we need to distinguish between resuscitation, reincarnation and resurrection.

Resuscitation is bringing someone back to life. With medical science as it is now, it is quite common for people to die and be brought back to life. I have a book at home which is the life story of Tom Scarinci, an American Italian. We were ministering in Berlin and he spoke first. He just got up and said, "I was dead for ten days and Jesus raised me from the dead." I was the second speaker and I thought, 'Follow that!' He then proceeded to tell of the most amazing resuscitation I had ever heard about.

It took place in Stanford Medical Center, which was attached to Stanford University in San Francisco, where Tom died for ten days and his brain was starved of oxygen, though his body was kept going by an oxygen pump for his lungs, and a heart pump. Nevertheless, he was clinically dead for ten days — and raised. It was one of the funniest stories I have heard, and one of the most amazing. His book, *Ten Days Dead*, has on its cover a picture of his body as it lay for those ten days.

That is resuscitation because that man will die again. He was brought back into the old body and, while that is a wonderful thing to do, he still has old age and death to face.

That applies to almost all the raisings of the dead in the Bible except one — that of Jesus. Lazarus died again; in fact there is a legend that he was never able to smile again because he was back into this sinful world for the rest of his life.

Most of us now know about the 'kiss of life' and what we should do when someone has drowned. In hospitals there are many resuscitations. People may be brought back to life with electrical shocks to the heart and so on. So that is resuscitation. It is not resurrection because Jesus did not 'come back to life' like that, he went on to something quite new and he is still alive two thousand years later. That did not apply to any of the other 'resurrections' in the Old or New Testaments. The others all came back into their old bodies, back into the old world, and all died again—that is not resurrection really. Resurrection is getting a new body that will not grow old and not die and not be diseased and not be weak and tired.

What about the Eastern idea of *reincarnation*? It is a belief that you come back in another body, and whether it is a better or worse life depends on how you did the previous time. You go on coming back in different bodies – as different people, or even animals – until, finally, if you have been good all the way through, you are rescued from your body altogether and can live without a body for the rest of eternity. That is totally different from resurrection.

In *resurrection* you come back as yourself with a new body that will not grow any older or die—an immortal body; the kind of body that God wanted you to have in the beginning. That is a totally different thing and you don't finally escape the body, you live in your new body forever. I am looking forward to getting my new body because I have a theory and it was shared by many Christians through the ages, namely that one day my body (like his body) will be thirty-three. I can't wait to be thirty-three again! That was when I was my best — physically, mentally, emotionally.

When I went into that Temple in the Strand in London where the Crusader knights are buried, I was fascinated to look at all their marble effigies lying on tombs because they are all thirty-three years old even though they were matured when they died in battle. They too believed that they would have a body like Jesus, because Jesus has had no birthdays since the resurrection. He hasn't got any older, and we shall have a glorious body like his that doesn't get older. Think of it — never celebrate a birthday again! Don't worry, you will be happy about that!

Hebrew and the Greek views of life after death could not have been more different. We are brought up on Greek thinking, and in Greek thinking the soul and the body are so different from each other. The body is imprisoned to the soul, and when the body dies the soul is released into freedom. Something to look forward to is finishing with the body. Nothing could be further from the Hebrew thinking. The Hebrew thought is: without the body, I am incomplete.

I may survive death as a disembodied spirit but I am not a complete person. Paul puts it this way: 'I will be unclothed.' He does not mean he will feel naked, but something will be missing from his consciousness. Therefore, he looked forward to the day when he would get his new body. That is why he says, 'Sometimes I think I don't want to enter the disembodied state.' He thinks again and says, 'No, I'd rather be absent from my body and at home with the Lord.' That is far better than this life, but nevertheless he clearly feels as a

Hebrew, as a Jew, that life is not complete unless you have a body and that is somehow part of *you* — not just something physical you live in for a few years.

When you look in the mirror and see your body, you are looking at *you*. To be with those who have died in Christ will be a marvellous experience; but we are still waiting for something more — we are waiting for that new body. You do not get a new body when you die—that will come later and will come to us together. Abraham will get his new body when I get mine, on the same day. Are you looking forward to that? We pass from death into the disembodied state one by one, but we get our new bodies as God's people altogether, at the same time. What a day that is going to be! Got a new body!

So Hebrew thinking about death was that it is a limitation, robbing you of your body. It is not oblivion but it is a disembodied existence. Therefore, God would complete our existence, giving us a new body. I can best explain it by saying that no Christian creed ever said, 'I believe in the immortality of the soul.' They say, 'I believe in the resurrection of the body.' That is the Christian hope for the future, not that like that song about John Brown, in which his 'soul goes marching on'. Your soul will be put back into a new body which will be much better than this one, and one that will do exactly what you want it to do, in which the body will be your perfect servant, whereas in this first phase the body is sometimes the master and controls us. The older you get the more it controls you, as I'm finding out. I never knew what old age was going to be like, now I know and it is different. It is not quite what I expected, but there we are—I am getting old.

Now let us look at the sequence of events in Jesus' life. He raised Lazarus from the dead, not many weeks before he himself died. That miracle was the talk of the nation because the man had been dead four days and when Jesus said "Open the tomb up," his sister said, "But Lord, by this time he smells." Corruption will have set in and you just can't do that. But Jesus said, "Open the tomb up." The next thing they saw was Lazarus standing at the mouth of the tomb still wrapped up in the clothes because he was being brought back into his old body, not resurrected in his new body. He had to be unwrapped to set him free to move. Jesus said, "Let him loose." Take the clothes off so he can move — because they could see his face and his eyes open, but he couldn't move. So Jesus said, "Unwrap him and let him go," which they had to do. They never had to do that with Jesus because he did not come back into the old body. The old body actually disappeared, simply ceased to be, and the result was that the body and bandages simply collapsed flat and the head bandage was simply left rolled up by itself. When John the apostle saw that, the Bible says, "He believed." We don't know quite what he believed, but he said he believed that no man had taken that body. You couldn't get a body out of those clothes and keep them wrapped up. John believed that something supernatural had happened in that tomb.

We have already thought about the description of the death of Jesus and the duration of his burial. Now let us look at the account of his resurrection—as much as possible from a human point of view. I find it very interesting that they were shown the initial evidence for his resurrection before they met him. In this we see a very delicate preparation for people for what must have been the most astounding thing they had ever heard or encountered. So, in his wisdom, the Lord allowed them to see the evidence of his absence from the tomb before they had any evidence of his presence outside it. They were allowed to see the empty grave clothes; they were allowed to see the empty tomb. They were even told by angels, "Why have you come here? He's not here. He's risen." So don't come and anoint a body that doesn't exist! The big question is: who rolled the stone away?

When the women came on Easter Sunday morning, it was the first time they could come when the soldiers had gone and when they could work. They came on the first working day so that they could anoint the body. It was only as they got near the cemetery that one of them said, "Who is going to roll the stone away for us?" If it took twenty men to push it there, could a few women roll it away? Never—but when they got there it had been rolled away, pushed over and an angel was sitting on it. Angels are stronger than we are and I think an angel just came and pushed it away, pushed it over and sat on it. I love that. By the way, the angel didn't roll the stone away to let Jesus out of the tomb. They only rolled it away to let the world in to see. So when the women came to the tomb they found it empty. They dashed back and told the disciples. They ran to the tomb, we are told, and still they were wondering whether somebody had broken in and stolen the body. When Peter and John arrived at the tomb, Peter (typically) ran straight in. John stood at the doorway and looked, and he saw those grave clothes and that convinced him. Nobody had moved that body—only God had been busy in that tomb.

Then the appearances began, and the first appearance outside the tomb was to a woman — Mary, not Mary the mother, but Mary Magdalene. She didn't realise who she was talking to until the voice said, "Mary." She recognised the voice — what a moment. Now we have a mistranslation in our Bibles. Jesus did not say to her, 'Don't touch me.' He said, "Stop touching me; don't hold on to me." She had obviously got hold of his ankles and said, "I'm not going to let you go ever. You're back and I'm going to hold on to you forever." He said, "Stop holding on to me Mary, I'm going back to heaven where I belong and you can't hold me here." It is a very touching scene because women who have been bereaved want a body, even a dead body. One of the tragedies of oil rigs being burned up in fire is that the bereaved have no body to bury and that hurts them. Women want a body to bury and honour, and in many cases they don't get one. Mary wanted that body and she wanted to hang on.

So, from then on, not only did they have the evidence of his absence from his tomb – and the empty tomb is a crucial piece of evidence and no one has ever been able to find the body of Jesus anywhere – but we also as believers have a disadvantage. Unbelievers cannot produce his body and neither can we. I used to wish that Jesus had stayed around. It would be so much easier to evangelise and say to your friend, "George, come and meet Jesus; George, this is Jesus; Jesus, this is my friend George." I know that when George looks into those eyes, he'll be a goner and he will belong! I can't do that, but when I grew up I stopped thinking in that childish way because if Jesus was still on earth and had not ascended to heaven, how often could you persuade him to visit your church? How often could you have Jesus in a service of worship? Maybe once in a lifetime. You see the problem? How often can you have his Spirit present?

All the time—every time you worship. That is why Jesus said, "I must go and send someone else in my place who will stay with you."

So we have a series of appearances. The book of Acts says, "He showed them with proofs that he was alive." Those appearances were real proof. There were two walking to Emmaus that night; they were not close relatives, nor were they close disciples. They were walking back home to Emmaus, about nine miles down the hill from Jerusalem, late that Easter Sunday evening. Now they were looking into the sunset and they certainly never expected to see Jesus. So I can understand that when a stranger said, "May I walk with you?" they didn't recognise him; they were never really close to him anyway, though they were related. As they talked he said, "Why are you looking so miserable?" They said, "Haven't you heard? The one we hoped was going to rescue Israel is dead—they killed him." Then he gave them a Bible study. He said, "Oh you fools, don't you know your Bible?" He took them right through the Old Testament, the first five books, the Law and the Psalms and the Writings and then the Prophets, and he showed them everything about himself and said, "Didn't you realise that glory comes through suffering?" That he had to suffer first before entering into his glory—it's all written in the Bible for you, why didn't you believe it? Still they didn't see who it was, and by now it was dark and they arrived at their home in Emmaus.

Somehow they didn't want to let him go but he made as though he would go further and went on walking down the hill, and they said, "Stop, come and stay with us the night. Let's talk some more. Come on in." Then they sat down to a meal and I always used to wonder how they knew. But you see it was the custom in their culture to ask the guest to break bread so that he could have the biggest piece. That is courtesy. So they gave him a loaf of bread to break for them and his hands came out, and they saw. Their eyes were opened and they knew! They were so excited they got up that same hour and ran nine miles uphill and Jesus got there before them because in his new body he could move more quickly than they. They ran back to tell the disciples, "We've had him in our house. He had a meal; he broke bread." Then a voice said, "Shalom." The first word the risen Jesus said was "Shalom" (peace), and they knew he was alive. They just could not believe it that he was back and so they were having fish and chips for supper. So he said, "Give me some." And they gave him some and he ate before them. They thought, 'He's got to be real; ghosts don't eat your food.' Finally they were convinced but still he said, "Look, if you don't believe it, come and put your finger through my hands. Put your hand up here in my side." Now the body was a new body but it still bore the identification marks of his old body—that is an important point. He was still recognisable by those scars. His new body had them and so he gave proofs that he was alive.

Later, he met them in Galilee, cooked breakfast for them and roasted some fish. It is all terribly real. These are not ghost appearances, these are not spirit appearances; this is a *re-embodied* spirit. Yet it is a body that could disappear at will and appear at will. It is a body that could pass through locked doors, both ways, in and out. It is a unique body with greater powers; things that Jesus never did in his old body, he was able to do in his new body. But one thing he was never able to do was to be in two places at once. It was either in Jerusalem or up in Galilee or in Emmaus. He could travel swiftly from one to the other but he never appeared in more than one place at once.

That is an important point because bodily (when we are embodied) we cannot be in more places than one — even in his resurrection body Jesus couldn't. Now as well as the appearances he made, he made frequent disappearances. You would have thought that when he came back to them, he would have stayed with them visibly but he didn't. In Emmaus after they had recognised him because they saw his hands breaking the bread, he immediately disappeared. When he appeared to the disciples, he disappeared. Thomas – 'doubting' Thomas we call him quite wrongly – had, I think, more faith than the others. When he came back to them, having been off wandering by himself on the Easter Sunday evening, they said, "He's alive and he has eaten fish. Look at that plate with the fish bones on it! He ate our supper." Thomas said, "Unless I put my finger in his hands and my hand in his side, you're not going to catch me believing." One week later, suddenly there's Jesus among them again and he says, "Thomas, come and put your finger through my hand." Do you realise the significance of that? Jesus is quoting Thomas' words uttered when Jesus was apparently not in the room and he was now quoting them against him.

What the *disappearances* mean is that Jesus didn't leave them when they couldn't see him. He was still with them, listening to their conversations but invisibly. He was preparing them for an invisible presence. So he didn't just appear to them to prove he was back, but he disappeared from them regularly and convinced them that he did not leave them when he disappeared. Gradually they got used to his invisible presence and it was all preparation for the future. It is an intriguing thing. Wasn't Jesus a great teacher that he should teach them that he was there listening to them when they could not see him? So in all the appearances and disappearances he was more with them invisibly than visibly after the resurrection. He could make his body invisible and intangible, or tangible and visible. His body was a new body in perfect control of his spirit and that is what our new bodies will be. He could travel from Jerusalem to Galilee without a long walk in between.

When the disciples went back to Galilee, they didn't know what to do with themselves. Peter said, "Well I'm going back fishing, you can stay here if you'd like but I'm going back for a night's fishing," and he went back fishing, and then when dawn broke, they had caught nothing — but there was a man standing on the beach who said, "You're throwing the net on the wrong side of the boat. Throw it the other way." They did, and they caught one hundred and fifty-three fish. Now I have spent a night on the Sea of Galilee with fishermen throwing the net, and if you get four or five each throw you are doing well — but a hundred and fifty-three? You wouldn't believe what theologians make of that. One theologian said, "Twelve apostles squared is a hundred and forty-four and the trinity tripled is nine. A hundred and forty-four plus nine is a hundred and fifty-three." The way that some people treat the Bible! I will tell you what a hundred and fifty-three means: that's a lot of fish! That is all it means. Don't try and read any more into it. Those who allegorise scripture are on the wrong tactic. Take scripture at its plainest sense.

That was a lot of fish, and as soon as they caught the fish, Peter said, "It's the Lord," and he jumped into the water and splashed ashore. Then suddenly he realised that Jesus had lit a charcoal fire—that is a literal word—on which he was cooking fish for them. It was the second time Peter had looked into a charcoal fire. The other time was in the High Priest's courtyard when Jesus was on trial, already imprisoned, and a little servant girl had looked at Peter and said, "You have got a Galilean accent. You're one of his followers, aren't you?"

He said, "I never knew the Man."

"But I've seen you with Him."

"You haven't—you've mistaken me for someone else," and just at that very moment they brought Jesus through the courtyard and Peter wept. He had denied his best friend under pressure of course, but it haunted Peter.

Now he is looking into a charcoal fire again. Jesus said, "Peter do you love me?" There is very interesting interplay here—Peter refused to use the word *agape*, which is what Jesus used.

Peter said, "I like you," using another word.

"Peter, do you love me more than these?"

Peter says, "Jesus you know I like you so much."

"Peter, you just like me?" the Lord says.

Peter replied: "You know me; you know I'm very fond of you." He wouldn't use that word 'love' because he remembered the three times he denied Jesus by a charcoal fire, and now Jesus is healing that wound. He asks him three times and Peter refused to admit that he loved Jesus with the same love that Jesus had for him. He was honest, and because of his honesty Jesus said, "Feed my sheep." Peter became not the first pope but the first pastor of the Christian church, and looked after the flock of Jesus. It is a lovely scene. If you go there today to the very place where it happened, there are three stones set in the pebble beach, each in the shape of a heart. You can look and remember that Jesus asked him the three questions which neutralised the wound in his heart for denying him three times—it is a most amazing account.

These appearances, these disappearances, were preparation for the day when Jesus would go back to heaven — and yet Jesus had made a promise that it seemed he could not keep. He said, "Lo, I am with you always even to the end of the age but I'm going back to heaven now." That doesn't make sense, does it? Until you have realised that the Holy Spirit is the Spirit of Jesus, his invisible presence. So he promised that he would stay with them forever, just before they saw him go to heaven. Yet they weren't unhappy because they knew when he made a promise he kept it, and he said, "I'll send someone else to take my place, someone just like me, another comforter."

I don't like that English rendering 'comforter'. It speaks to me of knitted, woven vests and things like that. The word really means 'stands by' — someone to stand by you, someone to make you strong by being with you when you are in a tight corner. It is a lovely word 'stand by', and Jesus said I will send you another 'stand by' who will stay with you, and there are two Greek words for 'another'. One means 'another different kind' and the other means 'another of exactly the same kind'. When Jesus promised them another 'stand by' he meant of the same kind as me. So that even though Jesus left them and went to heaven, they were not unhappy. They didn't shed tears because they had Jesus' promise of another 'stand by' who would be with them all the time — who would be Jesus' other 'self', if you like, just like Jesus to them. When the Holy Spirit fills you, it feels just like Jesus is filling you because he is the Spirit of Jesus.

Let us move on to what I call the evidence for the resurrection. I have been talking about the sequence of events to show what actually happened, and you notice that Jesus never appeared to his enemies. He never appeared to Pontius Pilate, He never appeared to Annas and Caiaphas. So, although they heard that he had risen, they never had any proof given to them. Jesus does not give proof to unbelievers. He uses proof to those committed to him, and we know that Jesus is alive. He has proved it to us but he doesn't do that to the world. They must come by faith first and believe that he really does exist and that he is really alive, and then he will prove it to them — that was his careful selection. He appeared to the disciples, to the two relatives on the road to Emmaus who clearly hoped that he would be the redeemer of Israel; he appeared to five hundred people at once and it says, "Even then some of them didn't believe." Maybe some of the back of the crowd didn't get close enough and just thought they were seeing things, or that it was someone else, whatever.

We are in a different situation: we have no physical proofs; he has not eaten our supper. He has not told us, "Come and put your finger in my hands." That is why he said to Thomas the doubter, "Blessed are those who have not seen and yet have believed." We are in that category. We never saw, we have no proofs. So what evidence can we present to a world that doesn't believe? Can we present any? The answer is, "Yes we can," but it's not scientific evidence. Scientific evidence depends on two things: on an observer being present when it happens, and on being able to reproduce the event in the laboratory. No scientist was present at the resurrection and they have never been able to resurrect someone else. So we cannot give scientific evidence. You realise again that unbelievers say that Jesus is dead but they cannot produce the dead body. Believers say he is risen and we cannot produce the living body. So it looks like deadlock, doesn't it? But there is evidence we can produce and it is called legal evidence.

Every time a court of law meets before jury and judge, the legal evidence is the only evidence you have. Every court of law has to decide whether a crime happened or didn't, whether the man in the dock is innocent or guilty, and they do so on legal evidence. None of the jury was present when the murder took place. The judge was not present. They have to find out whether it really happened, and that could take days in a court of law. The evidence that is presented in a court, to prove beyond reasonable doubt that a murder has taken place, is of one of two kinds: eye-witness testimony, someone who did see things happen, or circumstantial evidence, in which the person did not see it happen but saw things that point to the fact that it happened. If you have no eye-witness testimony, you have to build up cumulative circumstantial evidence. You can build up a case for a murder having taken place, even if the body is missing and no one saw it happen, by circumstantial evidence. If you can produce enough of that, the case is decided and the guilty person is found guilty. The key phrase is 'beyond reasonable doubt'.

In the case of Jesus' resurrection, first we have eye-witness testimonies: five. We have the four apostles and their Gospels, and we have Paul. He was the first to give an eye-witness account of the risen Jesus, and four wrote it down later: Matthew, Mark, Luke, and John, and their evidence for eye-witness testimony is terribly convincing and I will tell you why. When five people have seen something and describe it afterwards, their description will not tally because each of them has seen it differently, and that is evidence that they really saw it. If they all give an identical account, you know they've cooked it up, but when the account varies, you know they really saw it. For example, supposing the court is examining a car wreck following an accident in the street: different people are called to court to give eye-witness testimony and they are asked 'what did you see?'

One will say, "Well, I saw a dog run across the road and the car swerved to avoid the dog and hit another car." Another eye-witness testimony will say, "There were two dogs chasing each other across the road." Well there's a discrepancy: was there one dog or two dogs? The answer is there were two, but one witness only saw one. Then what was the colour of the car? Well one said, "It was a kind of a bluey colour." One eye-witness says, "It was a greeny colour." The car was probably turquoise and one saw it as a green and one saw it as a blue. Now when you get those slight discrepancies between eye-witness testimonies, you know they are speaking for themselves and they haven't cooked up the story.

So one of the Gospels said there was one angel at the tomb and one Gospel says there were two: one inside, one outside. That proves they are giving a separate testimony — eye-witness testimony, for one only saw one of the angels and the other saw the two. Are you following me in this? It means that you have genuine eye-witness testimony when they don't one hundred percent agree with each other. When they do agree with each other in every detail you know they have cooked it up. They have agreed with each other.

There are discrepancies in the eye-witness testimony between Matthew, Mark, Luke, and John, which are exactly the kind of discrepancy you find with genuine eye-witness testimony. To me it is just an added proof that we have first-hand eye-witness evidences.

We were not eye-witnesses, but we have circumstantial evidence — what do we mean by that? Imagine that the case is one of murder and it is alleged that a man has pushed his wife off a cliff to her death. Nobody saw him do it and so now you have circumstantial evidence. What kind of evidence would convict him? Well, first an eye-witness says, "I saw him walking with his wife along the top of the cliff and later I saw him walking back by himself." That is not proof but it is circumstantial. Then they discover that the man had two airline tickets to go to another country and that he had a mistress and he was going to take her there. Again that does not prove he murdered his wife but it is circumstantial evidence — he had a motive. Then they discover letters written by that man to his mistress about his wife and saying, "I've just taken out life insurance so we'll have enough to live on." Now that doesn't prove anything yet but add it to all the other circumstantial evidence and the case is building up, isn't it? You can build up a solid case on that kind of evidence without having a body and without anyone having seen it take place, but a jury can decide beyond reasonable doubt he did it. Now that is one kind of evidence we have.

Let us take some of the circumstantial evidence for Jesus' resurrection. First, Jews changed their worship day from Saturday to Sunday — and that's unheard of. It is like persuading a Muslim to change from Friday to Saturday, or a Christian from Sunday to Monday. The fact is that Jews began to worship God on a Sunday, the first working day of the Jewish week.

Once I announced to my church that the elders had had a long discussion and we had decided to move our Sunday worship to Monday. I said, "Because it's Monday and a working day, we have decided to make the morning service at six o'clock in the morning and the evening service at seven o'clock in the evening." I managed to keep a straight face and they believed me! They were thinking: 'Well, how does that fit in with my domestic programme?' I am a bit of a tease! Do you know what they did once to get back at me? They didn't put a clock in the pulpit, they put a calendar there instead, to tell me when Sunday was finished! As my wife says, "Generally speaking, David is." You can think that one through!

For Jews to change their worship day from Saturday to Sunday, the first working day of the week – and meeting earlier and later because it was a working day – was unprecedented, and something must have happened for them to have made that change.

Take another piece of circumstantial evidence that you have to explain. Here are a bunch of followers of Jesus, hiding behind locked doors, scared for their lives, and weeks later they are out on the streets accusing the people of Jerusalem of killing their Saviour. How do you explain such an extraordinary change? Something happened that turned them from cowards into courageous men who were risking their lives in this way.

If the resurrection is not true but a fraud, how do you explain that two thousand years later fifteen hundred million people believe it is true? That is a lot of people to deceive, a lot of people to be taken in, and yet the majority of this world's population, at least openly and nominally, believe that Jesus has risen from the dead — more circumstantial evidence.

Whenever there is healing in the name of Jesus, that adds up to good circumstantial evidence. Many people have been healed of incurable diseases in the name of Jesus.

Now all this is beginning to add up, isn't it? I could go on and give you a dozen items of circumstantial evidence that would convince any jury in the world that Jesus is alive. This is one reason why so many people in the legal profession have become Christians. I have a book entitled *Lawyers Believe in Jesus*, and it is because they understand evidence. With an open mind, more lawyers have become Christians than any other profession because they have examined the evidence and are convinced by it. There were two professors of law in Oxford who decided to prove that Jesus was dead and thus finish Christianity off altogether, and this was in the year 1921. At the beginning of the summer vacation, they separated, each to examine the evidence and proof that Jesus did not rise from the dead. These were brainy professors and off they set separately for their summer vacation. When they met again at the beginning of the next term, one of the professors said to the other, "I'm really embarrassed to meet you because I'm convinced he rose from the dead." The other said, "You don't know how relieved I am to hear you say that, because I've examined the evidence and I've been convinced." The two of them got together in 1921 and wrote a book to prove that Jesus rose from the dead on the circumstantial evidence and the eye-witness testimony which they now believed. Another lawyer, Frank Morrison, wrote *Who Moved the Stone?* Do get hold of that book because he wrote it to prove that Jesus was dead and didn't rise, but he got no further than one chapter. He explains he had to write a totally different book because he had been convinced by the evidence that Jesus rose from the dead.

So why doesn't the whole world believe in the evidence? Because they don't want to — because if Jesus rose from the dead, he was right, not wrong. He was innocent, not guilty. Above all, if you believe that Jesus rose from the dead, you are going to have to change your life. You are going to have to listen to and believe what he said, and life is going to be very different. The world is therefore prejudiced against the evidence for the resurrection of Jesus from the dead. It is very difficult to persuade them to look at the evidence impartially—they don't want to. But I have found it is not the evidence that really does the trick, it is an *experience* of the risen Jesus. You can have all the evidence in the world and still not win your argument if someone doesn't want to believe. But, when they want to believe, they can have an experience of the risen Jesus. They won't need convincing after that. They have had a proof from the Lord himself.

Now we are going to look at the importance of the resurrection, and particularly its significance. What does it mean? What does it mean for us? What does it mean for the entire universe? What was God doing when he raised Jesus from the dead? I want to begin by saying that I believe that his resurrection body was not the body they put into the grave. It was a newly created body, and the old body had simply disappeared into nothing. God can make something out of nothing, and he can return something to nothing.

That is why the grave clothes were collapsed. That is why Jesus didn't need to be unwrapped from the grave clothes, unlike Lazarus. However, the body bore a resemblance to the old body. It still had the nail prints. It still had his facial features. It was recognisable, yet it was a new body. It was a real body—a tangible, visible body, but a body that could be made invisible and intangible at the will of the person occupying it. The reason why I believe that is because I believe the resurrection is the beginning of the new creation. The first part of the old universe to be made new was Jesus' body, and that was the beginning of the new creation. That is the significance for me.

Let me expand on that. I have said that I believe God created a new body for his Son within the darkness of the tomb—a body that was immortal; a body that would last forever; a body that would not grow old as his previous body would have done. Now I ask you a question that you have probably never asked yourself, but I am always reading the Bible and asking questions—I have got that kind of mind. I have never grown up, and it is just like little children saying, 'Why, daddy? How? When? Where?' Children are full of questions and that's how they learn — so I ask questions. The question I ask is this: where did Jesus get his resurrection clothes from? Did you ever think about that? You know that he left his grave clothes in the tomb. Did he appear naked in the resurrection? I think not, because it was a group of women who saw him first, and I don't think he would appear to them naked. So did he find a shop that was open and buy some clothes? Did somebody take pity on him, seeing this naked man, and rush home and get him some? The answer is that the risen Jesus got his new clothes from the same place he got his new body. It doesn't take much more power of an Almighty God to give him new clothes, as his new body. He was a new creation, a new body with new clothes.

Let us take that thought a little further. Do you realise that Easter Sunday was the beginning of the second week of creation? In the first week of creation God made the new heaven and the earth first and people last. In the new creation, he is making new people first and the new heaven and the new earth last. It is all in reverse order now, and the first bit of the old creation to be made into the new creation was his own Son's body. That is why it happened on the first day of the week, which was not a Sabbath, nor a holy day, but the first working day of the week. Everybody had gone back to work on the day that Jesus rose from the dead, and that was precisely why God raised him from the dead then. God was going back to work, and beginning the new creation with his Son.

Do you begin to understand? We are living in the eighth day of creation. God made the world in six days — whatever length or otherwise those days were I will not go into — but the seventh day was a very long day. It lasted centuries, during which God made nothing new, as the book of Ecclesiastes says, 'There's nothing new under the sun.' When you get to the New Testament, the word 'new', keeps appearing. It is about the new creation.

That is why we Christians do not worship God on Saturday. When the Jews worship on Saturday – the Sabbath – they are remembering that God rested from his work on the seventh day, and it is a day of rest for them. It is not a day of rest for the average Christian, it is often the busiest day of the week, because what we are celebrating is not God's rest at the end of his old creation, but that he has gone back to work, and started the new creation.

That is the profound *significance* of the resurrection. It was the beginning of the new world. It was the first new creation of God—Jesus' new body. And our new bodies are going to be like his glorious body. We are not an immortal soul trapped in a mortal body. That is the Greek view, which is still reflected in our education system. The Hebrew view is what Paul said in 1 Corinthians 15, that this mortal soul must put on an immortal body. When we put on our immortal body, then the victory of the grave has been swallowed up, and death has lost its sting. Read 1 Corinthians 15 very carefully. What God wants is to put a mortal soul into an immortal body, and that is what will happen. So Christians never say, 'I believe in the immortality of the soul.' They say, 'I believe in the resurrection of the body.' 'Resurrection' there means 're-creation'.

The beginning of the new creation will not end until the entire universe has died and been 'raised again' in a new heaven and a new earth. Jesus' resurrection is the beginning of a whole new universe. The God who made the old creation has gone back to work, so we celebrate on the first working day of the Jewish week, Sunday. Since the earliest days, Christians have risen for worship on a Sunday morning because that is the great day of God beginning again to work in creation, but this time a brand new creation.

The resurrection had more meaning than that. Let us go right back to the trial of Jesus. They found him guilty in the Jewish trial by night—of blasphemy. In the trial he had by day before Pilate, the Roman, he was alleged to be guilty of treason. We know that he was innocent on both charges.

He did call himself God, but was telling the truth. It was not blasphemy. He was to be the King of the Jews, but that was not treason, it was the truth. So what the resurrection is doing, first of all, is reversing the verdict of the human courts. It is God saying, 'You're wrong! my Son is innocent.' It is, as Paul puts it, God declaring that Jesus is his Son by the resurrection from the dead. That is at the beginning of his letter to the Romans. God is saying: you have been wrong to condemn my Son. He was innocent of all charges, and I declare him innocent by raising him from the dead. It was from that moment of the resurrection that the apostles, the disciples and all other believers were convinced that Jesus was the Son of God—and they were proved to be right. Everything he had said he was, was true. God has reversed the verdict of the human courts so that now we know who was right and who was wrong. It was Jesus who was right, Jesus who spoke the truth—not Annas and Caiaphas, not Pontius Pilate, not Herod. Jesus was proved to be the Son of God. Then, you may ask, why didn't God reverse the verdict earlier than that? Why did he not intervene when Jesus was being crucified and stop that punishment? Why didn't God step in? Even when the crowd mocked Jesus, and he cried out, "Eloi, Eloi, lama sabachthani." ("My God, my God, why have you forsaken me?") The crowd said, "He's calling on God, let's see if God comes and rescues him." Let's see if God reverses the verdict. But he let Jesus die. He let him be buried and didn't raise him until the third day afterwards.

Well, when I taught you about the death of Jesus I told you why. God wanted him to be punished. God wanted him to die. God willed the cross, and so the resurrection means that what Jesus did on the cross is now accepted by God.

Not only was his person vindicated, but his work has been accepted, and the resurrection proves that his work on the cross was accepted by God as a sacrifice for the sins of the whole world. Doesn't it all fit together beautifully? God knew what he was doing all along, and the time came after Jesus had been punished, after he had been put to death, to raise him from the dead and reverse the verdict. But meanwhile *he had been punished for our sins — he had died for us according to the Scripture.*

So isn't the resurrection meaningful? I have met Christians who think the only meaning of the resurrection is that we will survive death. No, it is far more than that. It is the beginning of a whole new universe, and what God has begun he will complete, but in reverse order to the first week of creation. I hope that next time you worship on a Sunday you remember some of this and say, 'Hallelujah! God's gone back to work! He's busy again. He's creating again, and I'm part of his new creation!' Isn't that exciting?

So those are some of the meanings – the significance – and because of all that and more, the resurrection is the foundation of our faith. So Paul in 1 Corinthians 15 makes a statement, spelling out the consequences: 'If Christ was not raised from the dead we are still in our sins.' The cross cannot do anything for you without the resurrection. That is what Paul is saying. If Christ is not raised from the dead, we are still in our sins — nothing has changed. The cross is of no effect. He died in vain if he is still in the tomb. Many people have realised this and seen how crucial the resurrection is to Christianity. Without the resurrection, everything falls. Our churches would have to close. We would have to admit to the world that we have believed a lie; that we had been deceived. We would have been defrauded.

Christianity would have to close down if Christ has not been raised from the dead. Many people have tried to say that it doesn't matter whether Christ was raised or not. 'He came as the perfect teacher and if only we all followed his teaching, the world would be a better, happy place.' We think of Mahatma Gandhi who was used to set India free from the British colonial power. He believed in the teaching of Jesus, and he tried to apply it, especially the teaching on non-violent resistance. That was the heart of Gandhi's life, and he attributed it to a minister called Stanley Jones, a missionary. The *teaching* of Jesus was all he picked up. He never picked up the idea that Jesus was still alive. He said, "If only we lived like the Sermon on the Mount, India can be free!" So he based his political agitation on the Sermon on the Mount and it worked.

What about the Russian Leo Tolstoy? He also believed in Jesus as a teacher and thought him the greatest moral teacher the world has ever known, and sought to apply his teaching, particularly in his novels. There are many like that in England who have a sort of Christian ethic – a kind of Christian way of life – who believe that the teaching of Jesus is good teaching and, 'We'll try and live by it.' There is only one problem with that: nobody has ever succeeded in living by the Sermon on the Mount. The standard is way too high for human nature. To acknowledge that if we did live like that the world would be a wonderful place is one thing; it is another thing to get people to live like that, because none of us is capable of doing so.

When Jesus made sin worse than crime, he pretty well damned all of us. He said it is a crime to kill people, but if you wish anybody dead, or called anybody a fool, you have murdered them in your heart — in the thinking of Jesus, contempt is murder. He said, "The law says you mustn't commit adultery, but if you've ever thought about it, looked at a woman and wished you could take her to bed, you've committed adultery." He made the thought and the feeling inside as bad as any outward action. That is the Sermon on the Mount — Jesus told you to love your enemies, pray for them. He told you to keep your prayer life, your giving and your fasting secret, and not to do any of those things in the eyes of men. "Let not your right hand know what your left hand is doing." I feel ashamed when I read the teaching of the Sermon on the Mount. You find out that you are really a sinner. The problem is we can't keep it. Without the resurrection all that teaching is useless, wasted. That is what Paul is saying in 1 Corinthians 15, and maybe that is why there is such an extreme reluctance on the part of people to accept the resurrection — even to look at the evidence and be convinced.

You wouldn't believe the number of theories that have been raised by rational people to 'disprove' the resurrection. There are those, for example, who say that despite the presence of soldier guards and a sealed stone somehow somebody managed to steal the body. There are others who say that when the women came on Easter Sunday they came to the wrong tomb. They had witnessed where he was laid. There was only one tomb there. How could they go to the wrong one? It wasn't a cemetery full of graves. It was one private tomb. Then, there are those who say that the resurrection appearances were hallucinations, and they just thought they saw Jesus alive. Actually, he had eaten their supper and he cooked breakfast for them — and hallucinations aren't usually preparing food for you or eating it! Then there are those who say that he only swooned on the cross, and think that somehow in the cool of the tomb he recovered — from the flogging to within an inch of his life; from having had no food since the Last Supper — and then, following all that, he managed to push the stone away. The whole thing becomes so ridiculous. Why are they so anxious to prove that he didn't rise? Well, I repeat: their problem is not a mental problem it is a moral problem. They don't want him to be alive because if he is alive they are now answerable to him. They have to change their way of life.

They have got to adopt his teaching and by his Spirit live that way, and people don't want to change. That's why they don't want to believe it — because it would affect them so deeply. It would also mean that everything he said was true because God had vindicated him, and one of the things he said was that, "Every human being will be answerable to me—I will judge the nations." It means every one of us, and everybody out there who doesn't come to our meetings, will one day stand before Jesus to be judged. It means that Pontius Pilate will one day stand before Jesus. It means Adolf Hitler will one day stand before Jesus, and Saddam Hussein. Everybody will one day stand before Jesus and he will decide their eternal future. That is what he said, and the resurrection proves he was right and telling the truth. People don't want to think they are answerable to Jesus. They hate the thought that he will one day say, 'How did you live when you were on earth?' But that's the truth.

I have lived long enough to know that if people are really determined not to accept the truth, they can find ways of avoiding it. They can get around it in some way, and some of the nicest, kindest people refuse to believe in the resurrection because they don't want to change—that's the root of the problem. Yet I have seen the worst men that I could imagine in my lifetime transformed when they met the risen Jesus — when they talked to him and found he was alive. That, for me, is the biggest proof of the resurrection. He is still doing things. In fact, it says at the beginning of the Acts of the Apostles, where Doctor Luke who wrote it is referring to his Gospel, "The former treatise I gave you and told you what Jesus began to do and to teach. Now I'm writing a second volume of what he has continued to do and to teach." Two thousand years later Jesus is still doing things. There are things Jesus is doing now that he couldn't have done if he had stayed on earth, and that is the subject of the next chapter.

5

The wonder of his
ASCENSION

Jesus came into this world in a different way to everybody else and he went out of this world in a different way to everybody else too. We thought about his birth – his arrival – but now we will consider his departure. We have noticed that, amazingly, he didn't leave this world until two months after he died. He took his body with him, which nobody else does, and he left this world while he was still alive. Nobody else has left this world in such a manner, which we call his ascension. Now the crucifixion, burial and resurrection of Jesus are central and fundamental to our faith, but so are the incarnation and ascension.

The incarnation *prepared* for those three things, the crucifixion, burial and resurrection, and the ascension *completed* them, when Jesus went back to heaven. The Church calendar has always included Ascension Day. Every Christian creed includes mention of the ascension, after the resurrection. Yet, surprisingly, the ascension is possibly the most neglected item in the creed. When did you last hear a sermon on the ascension?

It is so much part of our faith, yet it is neglected. Why? For one thing it happened on a Thursday. So Ascension Day is not on a Sunday and it tends to get overlooked. But then Christmas day is not always on a Sunday and we celebrate that. So I don't think that the fact the ascension happened forty days after the resurrection, and therefore midweek, can be the reason that we hear about it so infrequently. We would all rather say hello than goodbye. We love greeting people when they are coming, and we tend to be rather sad when they go. So we celebrate Jesus coming but we don't celebrate his going. Maybe it's because we don't like saying goodbye, but I don't think so because the twelve disciples were happy, or the eleven disciples, as they were by now, were happy he was going. They were filled with joy when he went. That takes a bit of explaining. So is it psychological, the problem we have with the ascension? No, I don't think that's big enough.

Our problem could be theological. The Western Church has always majored on the crucifixion and the Eastern Church has always majored on the resurrection. I must admit that I am 'Eastern' rather than 'Western' in that. Both Protestants and Catholics have so stressed the crucifixion that the resurrection has somehow taken second place, but in the East it is the resurrection that is the big thing, and on Easter Sunday evening on the streets of Moscow people greet each other with the phrase, "Christ is risen" and the response, "He is risen, indeed." It is the normal greeting in the streets, I don't think it is in America, but that's the way it is in the East. But neither Eastern nor Western churches have ever emphasised the ascension. They have said they believe in it, and it is part of the faith, but they don't preach it, they don't think about it — from one year's end to the next, from one Ascension Day to the next.

The church I go to completely ignores Ascension Day, and I begged them to let me preach on Ascension Day, a Thursday. They said, "We'll only let you preach if you write

down everything you're going to say for our approval."
Well, I was so desperate to preach on the ascension I wrote
it all out for them and they let me preach. But really, it is
extraordinary. I think the real reason is what I call, not
psychological, not chronological, not theological, but
cosmological—because we can't imagine where heaven is.
We now know much more about the world and our earth and
its place in space, and the ascension doesn't seem to fit the
way we think about our cosmos.

Let me try to explain that: when people believed the earth
was fixed and flat, heaven was above and hell was below. Life
was very simple. Jesus ascended to heaven 'up there'. They
didn't know in those days that the earth is spinning around
so fast as it travels through its orbit. If heaven is straight up
from Jerusalem, then where is straight up from Jerusalem
when Earth is spinning? With all those stars spinning around
in ellipses, where do you put heaven? And where did Jesus
go? And where is he now? Did he just disappear when he
got as far as the clouds? We have all these questions, and
more and more Christian scholars are saying the story of the
ascension didn't happen — that it is a myth, a story with
a message but not true historically. Well, I don't believe it
is a myth.

When the first Russian went up into space he came back
and made a joke. He told the Russians, "I didn't see any
angels." Well that's true, he didn't, but they saw him. I think
it was more true when an American astronaut was asked,
"Did you meet God up there?" when he got back from space.
He said, "No, but if I'd taken my space suit off I would've"
— which was very true. But the simple thing is that science
has not found any sign of life outside of Earth. They have

hoped to find it; they have set up their radio telescopes, hoping desperately to get a message from out there. They have left tablets on the moon, hoping that somebody out there will pick them up and understand the message. The human race is getting very lonely, have you noticed?

We are desperate to find somebody else out there, but according to the Bible 'out there' is not empty space, it's full of life. The trouble is that science doesn't have the right instruments to see what's out there, and nor do we. We look into space—I have sat in the crater of a large telescope and looked around the heavens and I didn't see any sign of life at all, but I knew it was full of life—the Bible says so. There were angels up there, thousands of them. Yes, the Russian astronaut didn't see them, but they saw him. The fact is that there is another layer of reality we cannot see with our senses. All scientific instruments are simply an extension of our senses – sight, hearing, or whatever – to enable us to have a sensory picture of what lies beyond.

My answer is that heaven is everywhere except earth. That is how the Bible seems to think — it's always thinking of earth and heaven as if there is nothing else. Fortunately, science is beginning to come round to this with the advent of what is called Quantum Physics, which was pioneered by a German called Max Planck. A very clever scientist, he has introduced ideas that forty years ago science could not have accepted. He is now teaching that two physical objects can occupy the same space without being aware of each other—that solid objects can pass through solid objects and appear somewhere else. Now this kind of thinking to our 'popular science' minds is ludicrous but Quantum Physics is beginning to see a whole new pattern in the universe and believe that there can be things in your space that you cannot see or be aware of, but the Bible has been saying this.

There was a prophet Elijah and he was trapped in the city of Dothan. A young man, who was his assistant, woke up early one morning, looked out and saw the Syrian chariots all around. The city was completely surrounded. He said, "Elijah, look! They've got us covered! We're surrounded by chariots!" Elijah just said, "Lord, open his eyes, please," and he looked again and saw the chariots of heaven completely around the city, just above the Syrian chariots. It was a rare gift of God to see the invisible, and to see the life that's there already, of which we are not aware. The young man was ashamed of himself and he realised there were more heavenly chariots than Syrian. So there was no problem, no worry. He just saw as everybody sees and he was worried, but as soon as God opened his eyes he realised the situation was totally different. I think sometimes we panic because we are only seeing what's happening in the world that everybody else sees; if only we could see God's point of view and see what's happening in his sight. God is still on the throne. He is at peace, not worried about what is happening. It's all going his way and he will end it all. When we read all the stark headlines in the press we get panicky. We say, 'It's coming to an end, it's dreadful!' Lord, open their eyes that they may see the real situation from God's point of view.

So I think that is why we don't like ascension; it doesn't fit our pseudo-scientific world. Where did he go? The answer is: He left the earth, and when you leave the earth you are in heaven. Of course, they were still thinking in those days of seven layers of heaven. They would talk about the heaven where the birds fly, the heaven where the clouds are, the heaven of the blue sky, and so on, up to the seventh heaven where God was. But in fact God is all around us. We live and move and have our being in God. So to ask where in the universe is heaven is the wrong question. We should be asking: where is the universe in heaven? That is a different question. Heaven is all around us and we are not aware of it. The angels are all around us; every service of worship held on earth is attended by angels, did you know that?

Years ago I used to preach to a congregation of one — just one dear old lady who always turned up. Even if the weather in the Shetland Islands was dreadful, with a gale blowing, she would be there. She always said to me, "Well, the Lord's here, and you're here, and I'm here, so let's have the whole service." I had to play the little harmonium for the hymns, I had to take the collection from her, I had to preach to her, and those were some of the best services I ever attended. But when I have spoken to a small number and somebody asked me how many were there, I say, 'Thousands.' There were thousands! When we worship God, we are worshipping with the angels. We may not see them. By the way, did you know that the angels study your hairstyle? When Paul talked about it being wrong for men to have long hair and ladies to have short hair, he said 'because of the angels'. They are watching you when you worship. They want to see men who acknowledge that they are men and women who acknowledge that they are women and we show that with our hairstyle.

The angels are watching us and the Church of England liturgy makes it quite clear. The liturgy for the communion service has a phrase in it, 'Therefore with angels and archangels we laud and magnify your holy name.' I have a lovely recording of angels singing while a youth group was singing. Their song is just out of this world, literally — it is glorious music. Whenever you are singing, the angels are singing with you. Therefore with all the company of heaven we magnify the Lord, but we don't see them. Occasionally God gives us the privilege of seeing an angel—I had such a privilege just a few months ago and it is an awe-inspiring experience. God can open that other world to you occasionally, but it is only occasionally. It wouldn't be good for us to be seeing them all the time or we would stop being any use here. We would get preoccupied with that. One day we will join them and we shall see them. But God in his mercy and in his wisdom only gives us occasional glimpses of the world that is all around us.

Jesus just needed to leave the earth and he was in heaven — it is all around us; it is everywhere except earth. So he left the earth and went to heaven. A senior Anglican (Episcopalian) bishop in Scotland said on the BBC, "Jesus is not coming back because he never left." I am tempted to say, 'Rubbish!' The Bible presents heaven as everywhere else except earth. So Jesus had to leave the earth to go back home to heaven. That is what they saw him do. I talked about the disappearances of Jesus after the resurrection, but the last was not a disappearance because they saw him go. They only saw him go so far and then he was carried to heaven in a cloud, and he disappeared from their sight in a cloud. I can tell you now that the wind was from the west on that day because that is the only direction that brings clouds to the Holy Land.

So with the good westerly wind, Jesus simply rose and then was carried above the cloud. Since he was above the cloud at a certain point they could only see the cloud. They went on gazing up at the sky until the angels said, "Men of Galilee, why are you gazing at the sky? He'll come back and he'll come back in the same way as he went." If only I had a camcorder and had been able to film the ascension and then play the film in reverse, I would have a film of the Second Coming. But they didn't have camcorders in those days and nobody thought of doing it, but he will come back in the same way he went. Again, the forecast will be westerly winds and there will be clouds, and he will come back down through the clouds.

The universe is packed with life that is more intelligent and stronger than we are. God has revealed from heaven when he opens our eyes — when we need to see an angel to know that we are receiving heavenly help. Angels play a huge role in the events. If we don't believe in angels, there are whole parts of the biblical account of Jesus that make no sense. They were there at his conception, they were there at his birth announcing it to the shepherds, they were there at his temptations in the wilderness, they were there at Gethsemane, they were there at the tomb, and they were there at his ascension.

To show you how intelligent they are, they said to the disciples at the ascension, "You men of Galilee." They could not have said that a week earlier because one disciple, Judas Iscariot, was not from Galilee. So the angels would have got it wrong if Judas Iscariot had still been around. But they were right to say, "Men of Galilee, why are you gazing up into heaven?" because all that were left were from Galilee. I have just thrown that in. It is these little details that convince me that we have got a truthful record of the occasion; everything fits perfectly. Notice, in the account of the ascension, how often 'eyewitnesses' are mentioned. Five times in just a handful of verses:

> After Jesus said this he was taken up before their very eyes and a cloud hid him from their sight. They were looking intently up into the sky as he was going when suddenly two men dressed in white stood beside them. "Men of Galilee," they said, "Why do you stand here looking into the sky? This same Jesus who has been taken from you to heaven will come back in the same way you have seen him go into heaven."

Did you notice how often there is a reference to looking, seeing, sight? This was an event which had eyewitness testimony. It really happened; it was not a myth with a spiritual meaning. The disciples saw him go. That was not the way it happened before. For six weeks he had appeared to them and then suddenly he disappeared. He was trying to prove to them that he was still with them when he disappeared and was listening to their conversation. So though he disappeared he was still there with them. Now they saw him go, and that was very different from the disappearances. He did disappear into the clouds but they actually saw him go and realised that he was leaving them. They realised that he was not going to stay listening to their conversation anymore.

You would have thought that would have broken their hearts—having lived with him for three years, their best friend was gone. Yet they went back into Jerusalem rejoicing. They even went back into Jerusalem doing something that no

Jew would ever do—they worshipped him. Now for a Jew to worship a human being was utter blasphemy, treason. Yet they went back into Jerusalem worshipping Jesus. They now knew he was God, the Son of God, divine—fully divine. The carpenter from Nazareth with whom they had lived and eaten and slept — they now were so sure he was God that they were worshipping him. They were glad that he had gone back to heaven; they were rejoicing for him and for themselves. He could do far more for them in heaven than if he had stayed on earth, and I will prove that for you in a moment.

So when did he ascend? Forty days after the resurrection, ten days before the day of Pentecost. We celebrate Pentecost on Sunday but the ascension on Thursday. Where was it? It was on the Mount of Olives but just over the top from the city of Jerusalem. So it happened out of sight of the city. Just as Jesus did not appear to Pilate, Annas and Caiaphas, so at his ascension he did not want unbelievers watching. So he took the disciples up the Mount of Olives, just over the top, out of sight of the city, and from there he ascended to heaven. I am embarrassed to tell you there are now two churches on the Mount of Olives which celebrate the ascension. They each have a kind of plastic cast with his footprints in it to prove this was from where he ascended. Really, what Christians will do! But that's the place, certainly. How did he ascend? He didn't jump; he didn't spring up. He simply rose with his hands spread over them in blessing. When he got so high the cloud came and lifted him and carried him. That reminds me of a verse in the Psalms, 'He makes the winds, the clouds his chariots.' So he ascended to heaven—a real event in time and space. He had appeared and disappeared for six weeks but now they knew it was not quite permanent, but it was going to be a long time until they would see him again.

Such were the facts. What did it all mean? First I want to ask *what did it mean for Jesus?* The first obvious thing to say is that he was going home. That is a lovely phrase, isn't it? 'I'm going home.' Home is where you love the most, home is where your folks are, home is where you belong, home is where you feel relaxed — and Jesus was going home. When we were little children and had to go away, we went away to school or for a holiday. When we came home there was always a sheet of paper just as you came in the front door that said, 'Welcome home', and there was a drawing underneath about what we had been doing or something else. My father always pinned it up. So when he died I put on his gravestone 'Welcome home.' Lord Baden Powell, founder of the Scout movement, taught the boys how to follow each other, following signs. A sign might be an arrow this way or a line saying 'The wrong way', but then there was a sign that said 'I've gone home', and it was a circle with a dot in the middle. When Baden Powell died, that was put on his gravestone, a circle and a dot. Every Scout knows that it means 'I've gone home'. Heaven is home to Jesus; that is where he had been for so long. At the ascension he was going home. He had been away for thirty-three years.

Secondly, *he was going home safe and sound.* He had been in battles; he had taken huge risks while he had been away. He had faced great dangers, but was coming home safe and sound, beyond the reach of his enemies — safe at last. Thirdly, *he was coming home victorious.* The Roman Emperor would often send a son to go and deal with enemies in a far distant part of the empire. The son would come home victorious and the emperor would lay on a victory procession. In that procession there would be the victorious soldiers, the victorious son in his chariot, then the prisoners of war in chains, and then wheeled vehicles with all the loot, all the spoil they had taken from the enemy. That whole victory procession, would march through the biggest street in Rome. The emperor would sit and the crowd would applaud his son.

That picture is taken up in the Bible and it says that Jesus ascended on high bringing captives with him, giving gifts to men, the spoil of the battle. It is all there: a son coming back from battle victorious. Usually the emperor would then reward his son by saying come and sit on my right hand and the son would leave his chariot and climb the steps to the throne and sit down with his father. In fact it was not unknown in the Roman Empire for the emperor then to say, 'You are now the emperor. You take over the emperor's position. You rule.' Now all that kind of language is picked up in Paul's letters about the ascension. He was going home, he was going home safe and sound; he was going home victorious.

One can only imagine the welcome that Jesus received when he got back to heaven. We are not told exactly, but do you think the angels could keep quiet when he got back victorious? But actually what happened was that he was then crowned. The ascension is Jesus' coronation: when God exalted him and gave him the name which is above every name and he was crowned King of the universe—the coronation. You know that the British are better than anybody at spectacle. You have seen that the Royal Wedding was second to none and I make that claim— we can make the best show on earth out of a royal event. I can remember vividly the first time I had ever seen television, watching the coronation of Her Majesty, Queen Elizabeth—what a show that was! The golden coach is brought out for that, a coach covered in gold. It is a spectacle. Maybe you will see it in your lifetime — but it is very rare.

My father was a guest of the royal family at that wedding. I love to see the old films of it because I can pick him out, and I kind of feel I was there! The ascension was Christ's coronation day, and that is why we celebrate it. It was the day when he was crowned King, when all authority in heaven and earth were given into his hands, when he sat (and still sits) at the right hand of the Father and he took over the running of the universe. That is what the ascension means—he is King of kings, Lord of lords, President of presidents, Prime Minister of prime ministers—he is it. This is the great day when he ascended to heaven and sat down on his throne.

In Philippians chapter 2 Paul says, "God super exalted him." Not just 'exalted him', as our Bibles say, but the word is, '... *super exalted him and gave him a name above every other name, that at the name of Jesus every knee shall bow and every tongue confess that he is Lord to the glory of God the Father.*'

The saints from the Old Testament would welcome him, the angels would welcome him, the Father welcomed him, imagine the scene. It is not described for us; it would be almost too much for us, but I can imagine it. This was the great day to which Jesus had looked forward, and he endured the cross, despising the shame for the joy that was set before him, and the joy was the day of his coronation. He was looking forward to this when he went through the cross. It helped him through the cross to know that it was waiting for him afterwards. The government is now on his shoulder.

We need to remember an often overlooked feature—when Jesus went back to heaven he was different. He was not the person who had left heaven, he was now human. Can you imagine what the angels felt when they saw a human being made lower than the angels now reigning above them? Never forget there is now – there was – a human being in charge of the universe. He had come down, adopted our human nature permanently, and went back to heaven as a man. He is still a man and he is running the whole universe on our behalf. He is doing it for the church and he is doing it for the whole world and he is reigning now until all his enemies are beneath his feet—that is the objective.

There are still people who don't acknowledge him, still nations that don't acknowledge him, but he will reign. One of the most quoted Old Testament psalms in the New, in fact the most quoted text, is from Psalm 110: 'He will reign until all his enemies are beneath his feet.' That is what we are looking forward to. He is reigning already but there are many who don't acknowledge it. One day every knee will bow, every tongue confess that he is Lord. So there is a man in highest heaven who represents us there. Even more mysterious in a way to our finite minds, there is now a man in the godhead. Jesus has taken our human nature into the godhead. God is different—he was not like this before but now in the godhead itself there is one person who is a human being like us and he will remain that human being forever. When he comes back you will see a human being; that is the Son of God, the eternal Son of God.

That is what it meant for Jesus, but we are now going to move on from that. I want to look at the ascension from our point of view. What does it mean to us that Jesus has ascended? Well I have almost told you already—we have a human being at the centre of the universe. Talking to a Roman Catholic lady, I said, "Why do you pray to Mary?" and she replied, "Because she's human—she understands us." I said, "But don't you realise that Jesus is human and he understands us? He has been tempted just as we are. He is the best person we could have up in heaven pleading for us when we do silly and sinful things." It's a great thing to us that we've got Jesus up in heaven, that there is only one mediator between God and man, the man Christ Jesus.

We don't need anyone else; we have him and he is a perfect High Priest. We need a priest to represent us but we don't need earthly priests—that's a mistake that many churches have made. We are all priests. The priesthood of all believers is part of the New Testament teaching but we need a High Priest and we have one—and the best one we could ever have. We go through him to the Father when we pray. We say at the end of a prayer, '...through Jesus Christ our Lord', not because that is a kind of formula but because we are praying *through* Jesus. It is Jesus who said, "Whatever you ask in my name I will give it to you." So our prayers are taken by Jesus as our High Priest and presented to the Father. Could we have a better one who understands us perfectly, who has been through it all, as we go through it all? He understands and he represents you.

When a Christian sins, two things happen in heaven: the first is there is one person in heaven who accuses us, the accuser of the brethren. Don't think Satan is in hell, not yet—he is in heaven. He accuses the brethren in heaven. In the heavenly council he said, 'One of your people has sinned!' But the same New Testament that tells us that he accuses the brethren tells us that we have an advocate before the Father and he represents us against Satan. So, whenever we sin, Satan jumps on that and says, 'There you are Lord—he is sinning, he is not holy.' The Lord Jesus steps in as our advocate on high. Read the first letter of John, the first chapter, which talks about our advocate. So we have an accuser and an advocate. You could not have a better advocate as I have shown in the story of the woman taken in adultery. Jesus is the best lawyer there ever was. Jesus can say, "Neither do I condemn you," and he pleads our case before God.

Furthermore, *he intercedes for us*. We tend to think too highly of our intercession, at least we are thinking too highly of it when we forget *his* intercession for *us*. When nobody else is praying for you, Jesus is—what a thought! He is the greatest intercessor there ever was. The New Testament says he is interceding for us before the Father. He said to Simon Peter, "Peter, I prayed for you." Just let him speak your name there and think of Jesus saying, 'I'm praying for you.'

'Oh, but Lord, I'm too busy interceding for a nation.'

'I'm interceding for you.'

Just remember that when you begin your intercession for other people—start by thanking Jesus for interceding for you and praying for you. That's just one of the things he is doing for you in heaven. As he prayed for his disciples on earth, so he prays for us now in heaven.

Let us move on and ask *what is Jesus doing for us now that he wasn't doing for us before he ascended?* Well, here is something you 'twits' can put on your Twitter, or whatever it is. Here is a sentence for you: when Jesus ascended to heaven he became a baptist. Let that sink in! There are two people in the New Testament called 'baptists'. One is Jesus' cousin John and the other is Jesus himself. In fact, both are described with the same Greek words, *ho baptisein*, which means 'he who baptises', and from that comes the noun 'baptist'. John was a baptist; Jesus became a baptist when he ascended to heaven. Let me explain: the word 'baptise' is very rarely translated into English. It is transliterated, so it is spelled in English letters, but it is still the same Greek word 'baptise', but what does it mean in English?

It means to be dipped, to be plunged, to be soaked. It means, basically, to plunge a solid totally in a liquid. It was used of dyeing wool. You took the wool and you plunged it into the colour dye, totally immersing it so every part of it would be coloured, and that was called 'baptising' wool. It was used of taking a cup and dipping it into a punch bowl of liquid to get a drink. You put the cup down into the liquid and brought it up full of the liquid and you had 'baptised' it. When you hear of a ship being 'baptised', that does not refer to it being launched with a bottle of Champagne broken over its bows, and 'God bless all who sail in her' and all that — that is not baptising a ship. It is when a ship is sunk and goes to the bottom of the ocean, that is when the Greek newspapers say 'Ship baptised'. It always means to plunge a solid totally in a liquid — that is the meaning of the word.

John dipped people into water, totally. Therefore, he was nicknamed 'John the plunger', or 'John the dipper', or 'John the soaker', or 'John the baptiser'. He it was who said, "There is someone coming after me that won't plunge you into water, but he will plunge you into the Holy Spirit; he will soak you in the Holy Spirit; he will dip you in the Holy Spirit." When Jesus came on earth he didn't do that.

Not once in his whole ministry did he ever plunge anyone into the Holy Spirit. The Holy Spirit was with his disciples but not in them. That is what he said to them at the end of his earthly life, "The Holy Spirit will be in you when you are baptised in the Holy Spirit. When you are plunged, soaked, dipped in him." But he didn't do it, and when he went back home he still had not done it for anybody. He talked about living waters springing up inside people who had believed in him, but it hadn't happened because he couldn't do it until he got back to heaven and received the gift of the Holy Spirit from his Father to pour out on ordinary people like us.

Jesus said, "Stay in Jerusalem and you'll be baptised in the Holy Spirit not many days hence. Wait until you receive the power; wait until you're plunged, soaked, dipped in the Holy Spirit." It happened on the day of Pentecost. It could not happen until Jesus took his place in heaven and then he received the power of the Holy Spirit for others and poured it out on 120 men and women, including his mother. They spoke in tongues and they prophesied, and the Holy Spirit was now theirs. All the way through the rest of Acts, more and more people were plunged in the Spirit and dipped in the Spirit, and so the Church spread.

That was what I mean when I say when Jesus ascended he became a baptist—neither an American Baptist nor a Southern Baptist. He became a baptiser, and that title was given to him as well as to his cousin John. I can just see the Tweet now: 'Pawson says Jesus became a Baptist.' But it is true, and I like saying things in an unusual way because that makes you think, doesn't it? I wonder what you thought when I first said, 'Jesus became a baptist when he ascended.' But he did and he was now able to baptise people in the Holy

Spirit. He has been doing that ever since and he could only do it because he went back up there. Nobody could be filled with the Spirit on earth until Jesus had ascended — that is the truth. Because he is now pouring out his Spirit on people, he is pouring gifts onto people, gifts that they never had, supernatural gifts to do things they could never do before.

Jesus is now pouring out his Spirit and ordinary people are getting extraordinary gifts. If you think of your natural gifts you might be tempted to have an inferiority complex. Don't worry, you're a great candidate for baptism in the Spirit and you will find yourself doing extraordinary things, things that ordinary people can't do, because he is pouring out his Spirit and gifts. The greatest gift of the Father was his Son. The next greatest gift of the Father was his Holy Spirit. He gave us his Son, but without the next gift where would we be? He has given us of his Spirit, says John the apostle — what a generous Lord. In other words, the church was meant to be charismatic, which means gifted, a church of ministries that come from above — whether apostles, prophets, evangelists, pastors, teachers. I am number five in that list, a teacher but I am perfectly happy with being number five. Whatever, they are not graded. God gives different gifts to different people to build up his church to make it strong and healthy and able to do his work. Jesus even said to his disciples, "Greater works than these shall you do. You will do greater miracles than I have done." I am often asked, 'What are the greater miracles?' My answer is very simple: "You do all his miracles and then you can think about the greater ones. Don't bother to discuss the greater ones until you've done them all, and then you can move on to the greater ones." People are so curious mentally about the greater gifts that they don't even bother with the others. Do what Jesus did; go on doing what he used to do.

Secondly, he is not only a baptist but he is the mediator. He is the one person we need to act as mediator between sinners and a holy God. Somebody is needed in between, who can represent God to sinners and sinners to God. We all need that mediator. Because he is a man he is ideal to be a mediator between God and man. We need that mediator to plead for us because of the accuser of the brethren (Satan). We need an advocate and we have Jesus. Another title that is given to Jesus in the letter to the Hebrews, because of his ascension, is that he is our pioneer—our 'trailblazer' would be a translation. Now this was how America was built, with pioneers who went west and opened up new territory. Really the story of America is the story of pioneers who wanted to go further into unknown territory.

Jesus has gone as our pioneer. Do you remember I told you that God's order under him in his old creation was: angels, humans, animals? In the new creation that is going to be changed. Under him it is going to be: humans, angels, animals. Isn't that amazing? God is actually taking redeemed human beings and setting them above the angels. So the angels will become our servants and they will minister to us—that is your destiny in Christ. He has gone ahead of us as pioneer. He's the first human being to be above the angels and he is only there to blaze the trail for us to follow. If you read the letter to the Hebrews it is all about following Jesus to that high place in creation. Oh, we must prepare for our destiny. We must realise that we are being called above the angels, where he is seated, at the right hand of the Father, that is where we are going to be. So he is our pioneer.

He said, "I go to prepare a place for you." Has he gone back to carpentry? Is he preparing a house with many rooms? I don't know, I'll wait and see on that one. He is not only preparing a place for us but a position for us, and that position in the new creation is quite different from the old. He made man a little lower than the angels but we see one Man now above the angels, where we are going to follow, and God is changing the order of creation. Fourthly, I would like to say that he is our Ruler, our King.

First of all, he is *ruling the church*. Church is a very unusual body because its body is on earth but its Head is in heaven. Sometimes there is a medical condition where the head is unable to control the body and that leads to all kinds of trouble when the body won't do what the head wants. You get a diseased condition, but I am afraid it happens very often when the church decides what it wants to do and the Head doesn't want that. So even though the church is a body on earth it constantly needs to be referring to its Head in heaven so that it is a demonstration of the rule of heaven on earth; so that it is a clear demonstration of heaven itself — a colony of heaven on earth. That is his plan for the church and he will do it if we allow him to rule us and be our Head.

Secondly, he is *head of the world*. Paul goes on to say that 'He is head over all things for the church.' He is ruling the nations for the church's sake and what he does for whole nations he is doing for the sake of the church. That is a lovely truth. He is head over all things — nothing happens without his command. He is sustaining the universe. He is drawing the atlas of the nations; he takes territory from a nation and gives it to another, he is in charge. There was a little child on a train all by himself. He was sitting in the carriage looking quite happy and quite at peace. The other passengers in the compartment got a little worried about him; they thought he was travelling alone. They said, "Are you by yourself?" And he said, "Yes."

They said, "Aren't you worried to be by yourself?"

"No", he said.

"Why not?"

"Well," he said, "my Daddy's driving this train."

That's what you can say in a simple way: you are a child of God—you can say 'My Saviour is driving this train. He's in charge. He isn't surprised by anything, he's not lost control. He's going to bring all things together because the whole goal of history is that all things should be summed up in Christ.' Everything we do to help that to happen is taking part in the purpose of history. One day it will all be his and we are looking forward to that day.

I will give you my testimony. Quite honestly, for many years I was a 'binitarian'. Do you know what that means? I believed in two persons of the Trinity and I taught two persons of the Trinity because I knew them both—I knew the Father and I knew the Son. I was happy preaching a gospel that was all about the Father and the Son. I didn't like preaching about the Holy Spirit. I had to once a year because there was Pentecost Sunday in the church calendar and everybody expected two sermons about the Holy Spirit. By reading some books I managed to put enough together to keep them happy, but I was so glad to get back to the gospel the next Sunday — what I thought was the gospel. So I preached the Father and Son and God did honour that, because he does honour truth, but it wasn't the whole truth. In my postgraduate year at Cambridge I had majored on one question in my research: 'What happened on the day of Pentecost in Acts 2?' So I had written papers on this theme which got a good mark. I called it 'emptying the church by degrees'! I used to produce these papers and, if I put enough Greek into them and quoted enough scholars, they were accepted as good student's work but I didn't know the Holy Spirit and it bothered me. I thought, 'What is it about the Holy Spirit? I just don't understand.' Then I became a pastor. I still preached all I knew about the Father and the Son but it was binitarian, it was not Trinitarian.

One day I decided, 'I'm fed up with this problem, I'm going to preach about the Holy Spirit.' Well I announced I would preach twenty sermons on the Holy Spirit in one year. I would go through the Bible looking at every mention of the Holy Spirit and put those into my series of sermons. So I began with order out of chaos, looking at creation in Genesis. I went through all the tales of people like Samson and the prophets who spoke by the Holy Spirit, and all the amazing things that the Holy Spirit enabled them to do. I managed quite successfully to get through the Old Testament. Then I began on the New. I managed Matthew, Mark, and Luke quite well. I got into John, and that was beginning to get a bit tricky. I had arranged to reach Acts 2 on Pentecost Sunday. I thought, 'That's going to be so appropriate, isn't it?' But I still did not know what happened and all my papers at Cambridge had come to the conclusion that Pentecost was too far away for anybody to be sure what happened — in short, they were quite sceptical. Well, I remember I got to John 15 and I was beginning to get out of my depth, and I began to wish I had never started the series, but I just had to go on with it. I was dreading getting to Acts 2 and telling them, 'I don't know what happened.'

Coincidentally something else happened in the church. There was a man in our church who, every spring, developed hay fever. When the pollen count went up, his chest became congested with fluid and he became so weak that he was put to bed for anything up to six weeks until it had cleared. He was a clever man, in charge of a patent office in London — where you register a patent for a new invention. His name was James. Just at this time, when I got to John chapter 15 in the series, James developed hay fever, his lungs congested and he was put to bed and was lying there gasping for breath and he had a grey complexion. I thought I had better go and see him. I didn't want to because he was the unofficial leader of the opposition in the church. There is always one, have you noticed? Sometimes there is more than one — but there is usually one man who opposes everything the pastor suggests, and he was that man. Anything I suggested for the church to do that was different, he either opposed 'because we've done it before and it didn't work' or 'we've never done it before and we're not going to try'. Well that pretty well covered everything I suggested. I used to come home from church meetings really frustrated by this one man. I would complain to my wife, "Why did God send James to this church?" She would say to me, "Look David, the rest of the church is all with you, it's only James. That's just him, don't worry about one man." But I did worry about him because he just opposed me so often and you do worry about things like that.

On a Sunday afternoon I went to see him. All the way there I could not get out of my mind James chapter 5. Probably because his name was that, and I remembered it said, 'Is any sick? Let him call for the elders, let them anoint him with oil and he will be healed.' All the way there I couldn't get this out of my brain. When I got to his bedroom, and he was gasping there and lying back, he asked, "What do you think about James 5?"

And I said, "Well I have been thinking about it. Why do you ask?"

"Well," he said, "I've got to go to Switzerland on Thursday for business and the doctor has put me to bed for weeks. Will you come and anoint me with oil?"

So I said, "I'll pray about it."

That's a good 'get out', isn't it? I went home and tried to pray about it and I thought, 'I don't want him well. I've got a few weeks when I can suggest things to the church that they'll do.' I was thankful that he was ill and I said, "Lord, give me one good reason why I shouldn't go and anoint him with oil."

The Lord was silent, the heavens were brass.

By the Wednesday I was in quite a state but his wife rang up and said, "Look, he's got an air ticket for tomorrow to go to Switzerland. Will you come and anoint him tonight?"

By this time I couldn't think of an excuse and I had never done that before in my ministry. So I said, "Alright, I'll come tonight."

I went out and bought a big bottle of olive oil, and I called the other elders and said, "We're going to Jimmy's house tonight, to James."

We arrived at his bedroom but something had happened before we got there. I went alone into our church building and I knelt in the pulpit and I tried to pray for James. Have you ever tried to pray for someone you didn't want to be well, that you were glad was in bed? It is jolly difficult. I didn't know what to say. I tried to pray for him but I couldn't. I didn't want him to get better.

Then, quite suddenly, I was speaking a language I had never learned. It sounded like Chinese. Anyway, I prayed in this language and I remember looking at my watch and saying, "I haven't been praying an hour!" But I had. I looked at the watch and said, "I prayed for Jimmy for an hour and not in my own language. I wonder if I can do that again." I did, and something like Russian came out. I was praying for Jimmy with all my heart and I thought: 'This is what happened in Acts 2; this is it!' So I thought something was going to happen that night!

Some of the elders and I went to his bedroom and we opened the Bible at James chapter 5. We almost treated it as a car service manual—you know how you look for what you should do next. The first thing was confess your sins to one another. I thought we had better do that. So I said to James, "I've never liked you."

He said to me, "That's mutual."

We went through the book and then it said to anoint him with oil. So I got the bottle and took the cork out, and I went all over his head. Then we looked at the Bible and said "We've done everything."

Guess what happened? Absolutely nothing! He lay there, grey, and I just thought we had really blundered. I got up and ran away. Reaching the door, I turned back and said, "Have you still got your air ticket, James, for tomorrow?"

"Of course."

I said, "I'll run you to the airport." Then I ran, and thought, 'He'll be worse than ever now because he's not been healed.

Oh boy, it was bad enough before, but now I've made the situation ten times worse.' I didn't sleep that night, and in the morning I didn't dare to contact him.

I tried to go into my study and work but the telephone rang about nine thirty, "Hello, this is James. Will you run me to the airport at eleven o'clock?"

"James!" I said, "are you better?" I was totally surprised to hear his voice and it sounded healthy, no huskiness.

He replied, "Yes, I'm better. I've been to the hairdresser to have my hair cut to go to Switzerland. And the hairdresser said, 'I'm afraid, sir, I'm going to have to give you a shampoo before I cut your hair. I've never had such oily hair in my life.'"

So he had got his hair cut and then he had called me. I said, "But James, are you feeling up to it? Does your doctor say you can go?"

"Yes, I've been to see the doctor."

"What happened?" I asked.

"In the middle of the night it was as if two huge hands squeezed my chest and I brought up a bucket full of liquid. I can breathe!"

So I ran him to the airport. Now then, that man became my best friend. Not only that, but he and his wife got baptised in the Holy Spirit. Not only that—although he had had the weak chest since he was a boy, he has never had it again.

Well, I got into the pulpit the next Sunday to continue my series on the Holy Spirit. I thought I had just preached as I had done in all the previous sermons. I had prepared my notes weeks back. I just took the next study in the Holy Spirit in John as normal. I was not conscious of any difference at all. But a young man came to me afterwards and said, "What's happened to you this week?"

"Why do you ask?" I said.

"This week you know what you're talking about!"

That man is now a missionary working among Iranians, a young carpenter actually. From then I was in a new dimension of ministry and have been, I trust, ever since. I'm Trinitarian—I believe in Father, Son, and Holy Ghost. That is my testimony about that. I hope you have had the same experience and that you know personally the Father, and his Son, and the Holy Spirit. You are a true Christian, if so.

Let us return to the matter of the ascension. When the ascension is neglected certain things creep in that are not really part of the New Testament gospel. Once you believe that Christ has ascended and is seated at the right hand of God you no longer talk about 'Invite Christ into your life, open your heart and let Christ in' — as if little Jesus creeps into your heart. You thought of him as down here on earth living in people's hearts, but when you really believe in the ascension you know that he is up there, where his Father is, ruling the universe—you get a much bigger view of Jesus, not Jesus coming into me on earth, but reigning up there. It is his Spirit who comes in. Yet so often evangelists say, 'Open your heart and let Jesus in.' They will use a text that has no meaning for evangelism: *"Behold, I stand at the door and knock. If any man hears my voice, let him open the door and I will come into him and sup with him."* That is a prophetic word to a church that has lost Christ; it has nothing to do with conversion. But that text has been taken out of context. There are only two verses in the whole of Paul's letters that talk about Christ in you. One is in Colossians: 'Christ in you, the hope of glory.' The 'you' there is plural, not singular. It is not Christ in 'you, and you, and you,' it is Christ 'in you'. The other verse is, 'I no longer live but Christ lives in me.' It is very clear that in both cases Paul is talking about the Spirit of Christ—that's what is in us. But dozens of times Paul talks about you being in Christ, that is the major one.

Twice he does talk about Christ in you but he is clearly (from the context) meaning the Spirit in you. But all the other times he says a Christian is someone who is *in Christ*. When you became a Christian you were not saying, 'Christ, come in here,' you were saying, 'I am now in Christ.' That is a very different thing because it means that you are up there. You are seated with him in heavenly places. He is not down here, so if you are in Christ, you are up there. That has profound implications for the way you live.

As Paul told the Colossian Christians: 'Since, then, you have been raised with Christ, set your hearts on things above, where Christ is seated at the right hand of God. Set your minds on things above, not on earthly things. For you died, and your life is now hidden with Christ in God' (Colossians 3:1-3, NIV). Jesus said much the same thing: '"But store up for yourselves treasures in heaven, where moth and rust do not destroy, and where thieves do not break in and steal. For where your treasure is, there your heart will be also."' (Matthew 6:20-21, NIV).

Christ is up there, and when you come to be in Christ you're already in heaven, your spirit is. Your body may still be on earth and still be convincing you every day you are on earth, but actually you are now in Christ, seated with him in heavenly places in your spirit.

When you die you don't *go to* heaven because you are already there. What happens when you die is that your body stops telling you that you are on earth and your spirit realises where you are and where you have been for so long. For the Christian, death is already past, and therefore you don't go to heaven, you just stay there in Christ. All you are conscious of, all your spirit is telling you, is you are in Christ in heaven. So death is not to be feared, you don't go anywhere — you are in heaven already. That is the spiritual truth — your spirit is already there. The trouble is, when I wake up in the morning my body tells me I am down here, and if I am not careful I forget that I am up there. My senses tell me too much about my environment down here — listen to your spirit. That's why Paul says, 'If you then are risen with Christ, seek the things that are above, where Christ is, seated at the right hand of the Father.' That is where I am now spiritually. If I am giving a talk somewhere, that is the address of my body at the moment, but my spirit is hidden with Christ in glory. Amen!

When I come to die, my body will simply stop talking about earth to me, and all I will hear is what my spirit says: 'You are with Christ. You are in him and you have been in him for many years without fully realising it.' So Paul is constantly teaching: Seek the things above; live in Christ; live in heaven now; realise your spirit is in him. He is not so much in you, down here; you are in him up there. That is the truth you need to be constantly telling yourself, so that you live as if you are already up there.

So don't bring Christ down here; don't try and persuade people to invite Christ into their little life — bring them into Christ so they are in him. All this language – this jargon that we use in evangelism – you don't find any trace of it in the New Testament. What we find there is: Believe in Christ at the right hand of the Father, and receive his Holy Spirit on earth. They never say, 'Receive Christ.' They never say, 'Commit yourself to Christ.' They never say, 'Invite him into your heart' — all that is in language we have invented. They said: *Repent* toward God; *believe* in Jesus, *receive* the Holy Spirit, *be baptised* in the name of Father, Son, and Holy Spirit.

It is all there. Christian life was meant to be Trinitarian from the beginning. May the Lord keep us in that Trinitarian relationship, demonstrating what heaven is like to the earth around us, for his name's sake. Amen.

6

The wonder of his RETURN

We all have a fascination with the future and a fear of it. Just suppose I had a unique gift of the word of knowledge and could give you the date of your death. Would you come and ask me for it? Would you want to know the date of your death or not? You could then celebrate your birthday every year and your death date every year. Wouldn't that be fun? We have this fascination to know the future, yet part of us doesn't want to know the future — we are happy with the present. Broadly speaking, there are three ways to find out about the future.

There is the way of *superstition*, which is the occult way of finding out the future. That is anything from reading the lines on your hands to tea leaves in a tea cup, to tarot cards, your horoscope — all kinds of ways. Do you know that six out of ten men, and seven out of ten women, read their horoscope every day? That is why they are always in newspapers and magazines — what the stars tell you about the future. All those superstitious, occult ways are only ever at the most five percent correct, or as I prefer to put it, ninety-five percent wrong. So why people waste their time and money on such things I don't know. When I was in Paris I walked down the Champs-Élysées, the great avenue from the Arc de Triomphe, and I saw a huge queue waiting outside a shop. I asked my friend with me, "What are they

175

queuing for? What are they selling in there?"

He said, "They sell you your fortune for the next month for a considerable sum."

People were lining the street to get their forecast for the next month. It was pathetic, but somebody was making good money out of it.

The second way to foretell the future is the way of science. I was in a university not long ago, and there was a student operating a computer. I said, "What are you working out?"

He replied, "I'm working out the date of the end of the world."

"Oh," I said, "That's interesting. How do you do that?"

"Well," he said, "I feed all the relevant data from the present into the computer: population growth, food reserves, fuel reserves. All the factors I can feed in and then I ask the computer, 'When will the big crunch come when it will be impossible for many people to live?'"

I said, "Have you got a date yet?"

"Yes."

"What is it?"

"2040," he replied. "By that time so many trends will have crossed and the human race will be in real peril."

"That's very interesting because the Massachusetts Institute of Technology in America has come up with the same date from their computers," I replied.

Now of course nobody knows what different trends will come in, whether great disasters that reduce the population, or new discoveries of fuel or sources of energy. But on present trends that is the date that people are giving—2040. I don't need to worry about that! So there is the science of futurology as it is called, and now there are professors of futurology trying to predict the future, there are think tanks trying to predict—but science has never been more than twenty-five percent right about the future, and I say seventy-five percent wrong.

There is a third way to find out about the future and that's *scripture*. You can go for superstition and the majority of people do. You can go for science twenty-five percent. When you go to the Bible, it has been a hundred percent accurate about the future. There are 735 separate predictions about the future in your Bible. Twenty-four percent of the verses in the Bible have a prediction in them. Why do people go to superstition or even science when they could have such an accurate prediction about the future? One of those 735 predictions is actually mentioned in the Old and New Testament over three hundred times. That prediction is: Jesus is coming back. That is the most important prediction in the Bible when we are thinking about the future. So far, eighty-one percent of the predictions of the Bible have come true in detail, in practicality, literally. Therefore, I believe the other nineteen percent will come true in the future. The heart of those future predictions focuses on the return of our Lord Jesus Christ to planet earth.

So we are now going to think about that return of Jesus to planet earth. Then, since the Apostles' Creed on which we are basing these chapters goes on to speak about his judgment, in the next chapter we will think of that great Day when Jesus will judge the human race.

First of all, then, Jesus is coming back. There are many simple questions we need to ask about that. One: '*Who is coming back?*' The answer is the same Jesus who left two thousand years ago. In fact, the angel at the ascension told the disciples, "This same Jesus will come back." There will be no difference. He will be exactly the same as the Jesus who left. Therefore, he is coming back in his resurrection body, not his old one, and he is coming back as himself, and we shall see him exactly the same as the disciples who said goodbye to him on the Mount of Olives — this same Jesus, be in no doubt. In fact, he is the same yesterday, today, and forever. He is not coming back to any of the political capitals of the world. He is not coming back to Washington DC. He is not coming back to London. He is not coming back to Moscow. Nor is he coming back to any of the spiritual capitals of the world, whether Geneva, Canterbury or Rome. We know he is coming back to Jerusalem.

That makes Jerusalem very important. I go to Jerusalem or Israel for three reasons. I first went in 1961 purely to study the *past* of Israel, to see where the Bible happened, to take pictures associated with the events in the Bible to take home. I went purely for the past. I felt some of the sites were a bit spoiled by people in the present, especially people selling picture postcards. I regarded the people now in Israel as a bit of a nuisance. I was simply wanting to go to an open-air museum and study the past. Then in 1967 when I went out right at the end of the Six-Day War and was up on the Golan Heights, riding in an army jeep with an Israeli Army Major, I began to get interested in Israel *present*. For the next few years I went out to Israel to study the present — the amazing thing that has happened in the Middle East, turning a barren land into the most fertile land you could imagine.

Then, some years ago, I began to go for a very different reason — for the *future*. Now when I go to Israel, I go once a year for the Feast of Tabernacles to join thousands of other

Christians from 120 countries, and go to share with them the future of Israel. It is amazing to visit places where events are going to take place. So I don't take a camera with me now. I go to sites like Armageddon, for something big is going to happen there. Jerusalem itself, the city of the Great King, Jesus called it, and that is where he is coming back. So we know *where* Jesus is returning to us—it will be the same place and the same Jesus.

Thirdly, we know *how* he is coming back because it is all there in Acts: this same Jesus, coming to the same place, *in the same way* as he went. Not, I point out, in the same way he came the first time—it will be a complete contrast to his first coming. If it was a star that pointed out his first coming, it will be lightning from the eastern horizon to the western horizon that will mark his second coming, because again the sky will announce it. But that is a sharp contrast. When Jesus came the first time he came as a little baby. He is not coming back as a little baby. Though I was recently at a meeting where they asked me would I like a song after I had spoken. I said, "Yes, I'm speaking on the second coming. All you need to do is find a song about the second coming." My, did they have a problem finding one song about Jesus returning! Out of the hundreds of songs that have been written, there are hardly any about the Lord's return. Isn't that astonishing? But they did find one. In this song it says, 'We shall welcome him again as a little baby in a manger.' I thought: who on earth wrote that song? You know some of the songs we get today are rubbish, they really are, and that certainly was a good example of that. Coming back as a little baby in a manger? No, he is coming back as a full-grown man. All the world still celebrates Christmas and worships the little baby; they are going to get an awful shock when they meet him because he is not a baby any more. He is coming back as the Man, the Son of God.

If it is a contrast to his first coming, it is not a contrast to his first going. As he went, so he will return. There is a direct correlation. He went in the clouds, carried up to heaven; he will come in the clouds, carried down to earth. We shall *see*. That means again there will be a west wind on that day, bringing clouds from the Mediterranean. It is going to be a very noisy day by the way; if you don't like noisy meetings, don't come! There will be trumpets blasting and angels shouting. I won't be silent either! I have mentioned before that if I die before he comes back, I don't lose anything, I gain something. I get a front seat at the big meeting because the dead in Christ rise first. So I will see you at the big meeting, and what a meeting that's going to be — too big to hold in a stadium, so they are going to hold it up in the air, and there will be room for all of us there!

There are three Greek words used in our New Testament to describe the second coming of Jesus. The first is *parousia*. That has a very special meaning — *to arrive*. It is a word usually kept for a royal arrival. I was watching the news and saw that our Queen had visited the Republic of Ireland for the first time. There were an awful lot of security questions about that, but she was accepted very warmly. When she arrived at the airport that was a *parousia*. But the word has one or two other special undertones. It is the arrival of a royal person to visit a city, but the royal person will be met outside the city and then accompanied in procession into the city. That was what happened to the Queen in Ireland. She was met at the airport with the dignitaries and important people, then a procession of cars led her into the city. To let a royal person arrive at a city unaccompanied would be an insult. So they are always met outside the city, and then accompanied into the city. Then the general public can see them. It is very interesting that it is called a *parousia* when Jesus returns. We meet him in the air to accompany him to earth, when the public will be aware that he is back. It is a very important point—when we meet the Lord in the air, when we are caught up in what people call the 'rapture', we don't then go up to heaven we come back to earth with him. We accompany him on the last part of his journey—that is *parousia*.

The next Greek word used is *epiphaneia*. If the first word means to *arrive*, the second word means to *appear*—to appear publicly, where the crowds can see, where the public can know. Our royal family lives in Buckingham Palace. There is a big balcony on the front of the building and after any royal occasion everybody expects the royal family to appear publicly on the balcony where everyone can see them. That is an *epiphaneia*. Usually the wide road in front of Buckingham Palace called 'The Mall' is packed as far as the eye can see with people waiting for the appearance of the royal family. That's an *epiphaneia*. That is a word that is used of Jesus' return as well.

A third Greek word is the word *apokalupsis*. Essentially, that Greek word means an *unveiling*, an appearance in glory. Everything now visible that was not visible before, it is virtually a royal person with a crown and robes. It is an unveiling of the person as who they really are. One of the old fairy tales I remember hearing as a little boy was about an emperor who came a day before he was due to arrive.

Dressed as a beggar, he went through the streets of the town to see how people would treat him. The next day he came as the emperor in his carriage. The people recognised the face and realised he was the beggar from the day before. It is a lovely fairy tale. It is so true of Jesus. He came the first time humbly — only Peter, James, and John saw him in his glory, nobody else did. It says, 'The light was shining through his clothes, making him appear so bright and his clothes so clean.'

You can imagine a strong light inside cloth, it just lights up the cloth. They saw him in his glory and his glory shone through his clothes, but that was only one little glimpse and nobody else saw him like that until, perhaps, Saul on the road to Damascus. When he saw Jesus then, he was seeing Jesus who had returned to his glory and it blinded Saul, and he could not see a thing from that moment. But when Jesus gets back there will be an *apokalupsis,* an unveiling of his glory, and the world will see him as he is—in all his glory as the Son of God.

To summarise, we have those three very interesting Greek words on how Jesus will come back: *parousia*, a royal visitor being met outside the city by his important people, and accompanied by them right the way down to earth; secondly, *epiphaneia*—he will appear publicly to the people, and they will know he is back; above all, an *apokalupsis*—they will see him in all his glory. And we have answered our three questions: Who is coming back? How is he coming back? Where is he coming back?

But the one question that everyone wants to ask is, 'When is he coming back?' People have been trying to guess that date for so long. Martin Luther and John Wesley made guesses. Those two men were wise choosing dates well beyond their lifetimes — then they would never have to apologise to anybody, and eat humble pie for getting it wrong! Then we get people like Russell of the Jehovah's Witnesses, who said it would be in 1914. Miller of the Seventh Day Adventists had said it would be 1843. People have tried and tried. One I heard was 1996. Someone sent me a whole book proving that he would be back then. That correspondent hasn't been in touch with me since for some reason. Is Jesus going to come at any moment? Is his coming imminent? Could it be today? Could it be tonight? I have heard parents doing what I think is a wicked thing: telling their children, 'You had better decide for Jesus today because you might wake up in the morning and your parents will be gone.' I think that is a horrid way to talk to children and quite unlike Jesus.

Jesus said, "Watch and pray." What did he mean by 'watch'? The answer is he meant us to watch for signs. Those who don't watch and pray will be completely caught out. It will be a shock to them; they will be like the people in Noah's day—eating, drinking, marrying, and suddenly he is there. He will come to them totally unexpectedly, like a thief in the night, and they will find themselves facing loss. But the New Testament is quite clear that alert believers will never be surprised. They will be like the householder who knew a thief was coming in the night and stayed awake and watched for the first signs of the thief coming. So we are ready. That is why Jesus specifically gave us signs, signals of what is to happen before he gets here, so believers who are alert and praying will not be surprised. They will know as the events unfold that we are getting nearer and nearer to the time when he appears.

When the disciples asked Jesus a straight question, he gave them a straight answer. We have that answer in Matthew chapter 24. They said: what will be the signs, or the signals, of you coming? He gave them four, of which one and a half are clearly there in our world, which leaves two and a half to go. So we are not right at the end yet. The two and a half could happen quite quickly with the speed of world events, or they could take another fifty or a hundred years — nobody knows. But when the third and fourth signs come, we shall know that we are getting very near.

You will find in the middle chapters of Revelation a much more detailed programme of these four events, so you can take your pick. Matthew 24 gives an overview of the signs and then Revelation gives us the detailed view, but I am just going to give you the overview here because that will give you a general idea of what to look for. The signs have specific locations — the first sign is *in the world*, the second sign is *in the church*, the third sign is *in the Middle East*, and the fourth sign is *in the sky*. So you not only know what to look for, you know where to look. Jesus is giving us every help he can to be ready for the big event.

The first sign is in the world and consists of general disasters. Jesus listed three — wars, famines and earthquakes. We have all three in our world right now and we have had them for some time. I used to think that earthquakes were increasing, but they are not. What is happening is that far more people are being killed by earthquakes than ever before — partly because we have an increased population and partly because people are living in the most dangerous earthquake places in the world. They seem willing to build houses; they are hoping it won't happen in their lifetime and then it does. Earthquakes are happening now in places where they have not happened in a long time. So there has been an increase in that way.

One was in the centre of India where they had never had an earthquake, and it did a huge amount of damage. A building in which Youth With a Mission were meeting on an upper floor completely collapsed, but they were saved (their floor just ended up lower!) All kinds of stories circulate about earthquakes, but earthquakes are not caused by man, they are natural disasters. I have written a little book about this entitled *Why Does God Allow Natural Disasters?*

Wars, though, are caused by human beings, and so are famines. I was interviewed on Australian radio (ABC), and the very hostile interviewer said, "I've just been in Ethiopia, and I saw millions starving. How can you believe in a good God who lets that happen?" His name was Daryl Hench. I said, "Mr. Hench did you know that there is enough food in the world for everyone to have enough? The United Nations food organization has reported every year there is enough food in the world for everybody. It's not God's fault people are starving. It's that some of us live in countries where obesity is a problem and we are eating far too much, and others live in a country where there's not enough food. It's not God. God has every year supplied enough food for the whole world; it's we who don't share it out. We throw away food in our Western society that the third world would be jolly glad to eat. So don't ever blame God for famines. He is not at fault; he promised to do his part by maintaining summer, winter, springtime, and harvest, and he has kept his promise. It is we who have let him down, and keep too much food for part of the world, instead of sharing it out." So wars and famines are caused by human beings, but earthquakes are not. Get my little book on natural disasters for an explanation on why God allows those.

When the world is being shaken up by disasters, Jesus then gives a warning of deception. When each of these four signs comes we need to remember that Jesus said, "Don't be deceived." The deception when the world is shaken by disasters will be false messiahs. There will be people who will seize on people's insecurity, and make claims for themselves that are false. People will go after those who are giving false promises of security in a shaking age. We have seen that. When false messiahs set up, people, in their insecurity, will follow them. It usually ends in disaster, but nevertheless it is a feature of our world. Jesus counsels when the world is shaking with wars, famines and earthquakes, "Don't panic, don't be alarmed, don't be disturbed as other people are disturbed; don't let your heart be troubled." He says, "These are painful, but they are the pains of birth not the pains of death. They are the pains of a new beginning. Just as a woman experiences pain before the baby is born, the world is going to experience more pain before the new world is born." So when you read of these disasters in the newspapers, don't say, "This is the end," say, "It's the beginning. These are the pains of birth not the pains of death." That should mean you remain stable when your neighbours are shaken. It should mean that, but sometimes Christians get shaken. Jesus said, "Don't panic, don't be shaken." That is sign number one.

Sign number two is in the church. Just as he gave three things for the signs in the world, he gives three things for the signs in the church. The first sign is opposition: "You will be hated in every nation." Now that has never been true and it is not true now, but it is coming true. The world hates the church in many nations. It is a privilege to be in a nation where Christians are not hated; they may be a bit disliked, but they are not hated. Jesus predicts, in the second sign, universal hatred of Christians; that will lead of course to persecution. Now the majority of Christians are living in nations that are making life difficult for them. It is building up very steadily. I never thought I would live in England when Christians would be under pressure, but I do now. They are not just being laughed at and mocked in the media, for the first time in my lifetime English people are being arrested for preaching in the open air. That has never happened before in my lifetime. They are being accused of disturbing the peace, and with the new laws on what you say, we are losing freedom of speech. When that goes, Christians will be a prime target. So Jesus said, "There will be opposition to the church in every nation."

Secondly, he said, "That will lead to a great reduction in the size of the church worldwide." He said, "The love of most will grow cold, and they will leave." So the church will experience a great reduction in size. Some decades ago, in the days when Christians in Russia were under great pressure, there was a group of Christians meeting secretly to pray in a home. Suddenly, in the middle of the meeting, two Russian soldiers with Kalashnikov rifles burst into the prayer meeting and said, "We've come to kill you." The Christians looked up in alarm and then the Russian soldier said, "If you are not a Christian, get out." A number got up and ran. Then the two soldiers said to those that remained,

"Now can you tell us how to become Christians, please? We had to make sure of you first." What would happen to our prayer room if people burst in with guns? We don't know, but there was a reduction in that prayer meeting, and the true Christians stayed. Jesus said, "That's going to happen. The love of most will grow cold." Sunday Christians will be out the door like a shot.

Then, if you think that's negative, he said, "The gospel will be preached to every ethnic group." There is a logic that is illogical to us, but logical to God. A church under persecution that loses people will then be able to get onto the job of evangelism because it has been purified. Do you know how many church members in America it takes to win one person for Christ in a year? The answer according to the statistics is thirty-three. That is not real growth, is it? In England it is even more startling, but here is Jesus saying that once persecution comes and the numbers fall off, the rest will be able to do the job, and they will get on with it. The gospel will be preached to all ethnic groups, and then the end will come.

I can prove that to you. Everywhere in the world the church is being persecuted it is growing. It seems that persecution purifies the church and then increases it. It is an amazing story—the church is not being wiped out by persecution, it almost seems as if persecution makes it grow. So Jesus said, "Don't be deceived," but in the second sign he said, "Don't be deceived by false prophets."

In the world there will be false messiahs, and in the world people will follow them, but Christians don't. We know that Jesus is the Messiah, and we stay with him. But in times of pressure false prophets in the church can get a following among Christians, and Jesus warned us, "Don't listen to false prophets when all this is happening to the church." From our Bible we know what false prophets are. They prophesy peace when there is no peace. They say, "Everything's going to be alright, don't worry." They preach calm and collectedness when the church is in serious difficulty. So you can tell a false prophet — they comfort when they should be challenging. Jesus said, "Beware of false prophets when you see these things in the church." His advice is to endure; stick it out and evangelise while you endure. Preach the gospel even to those who persecute you, and endure. But it is in there that he says, "He who endures to the end will be saved." So each time when he gives a sign and tells us what it is, he then says this is how you might be deceived, and this is my advice. It is a very clear pattern.

So we turn to the third sign that he gave. This becomes more specific and it hasn't happened yet, and that is desecration in the Middle East—in Jerusalem itself. Here Jesus quoted the book of Daniel, and he reminded his hearers that Daniel talked about a horrible event called the 'abomination of desolation' in the temple in Jerusalem. Actually Daniel's prophecy has come true already, but will come true again just before Jesus' return. It came true with a man called Antiochus Epiphanes. He came to Jerusalem about 160 years before Jesus and did terrible things. He went to the temple and sacrificed pigs on the altar of God, knowing that they were unclean animals. He filled the temple rooms with prostitutes, he degraded the whole situation— fortunately, for only three and a half years, and then he was gone.

That was an abomination of desolation and Jesus said,

"The same thing will happen again towards the end of the world." He is referring to the Antichrist in Jerusalem, who will commit the ultimate desecration and claim himself to be God. That has not happened yet, but it will. He will be a man of utter blasphemy and terrible cruelty. Jesus said, "He will cause distress such as the world has never seen before." That will be a terrible but brief time. It is here that Jesus says, "Unless it was kept short no one would survive." He then gives a warning again of deception, and this time he says, "There will be false messiahs and false prophets." It is going to be a time when many people will be deceived, and we must listen to Jesus' advice, which is this: "Don't move unless you are somewhere near Jerusalem and then you should get out as quickly as you can." But he said, "The rest of you don't be moved. Don't listen to rumours. Don't let your ears lead you astray. Use your eyes and watch for these signs." Then he quoted a proverb, "Where the body is, the vultures will gather." That is a reference to the false messiahs and false prophets who come to eat the body of Christ if they can.

Then we come to the fourth sign, and this sign is unmistakable. All the lights in the sky will be switched off — the sun, the moon, the stars. The world will be left in total darkness. Who could mistake that sign? It is preparation for the lightning from the east to the west that will mark Jesus' arrival. But just as when Jesus died, the sun went out, when he is coming back the sun, moon, and stars will all go out, and leave us in darkness waiting for the light to come. Lightning from west to east will light the whole sky up. "When you see that," said Jesus, "when you see all these things...." At that point you will know that he is at the door just about to step through back onto the stage of history.

I remember when I was a boy being taken to the theatre for the first time. I forget what the play was; it may have been what we call a pantomime at Christmas. I remember sitting there, and one by one the house lights went down until we were sitting in utter darkness, but my little heart was pounding—I was waiting for something to happen. Then the curtains parted, the unveiling happened, and there was a brilliantly lit stage full of people singing. What an exciting moment that was. Ever since, I have thought that is what it is going to be when Jesus gets back. The whole universe—all the house lights switched off, and we are waiting in the darkness for something to happen. Then the unveiling, and Jesus in his glory lights the whole world up. Hallelujah! What an amazing event!

Will there be deception when the lights go out? It will happen too quickly. Nobody shall deceive us then, we shall be absolutely convinced he is about to appear. So what was his advice? None. The disciples were told to look up and wait, and Jesus would be there.

We have taken some time about those signs because that is what we are going to see before he comes. He said when you see all these things you know he is at the door. It is only when you see them all that you will know that. We haven't seen the whole church hated by every nation yet, so we haven't even got all the second sign yet. We certainly haven't seen the abomination of desolation in Jerusalem, and we certainly have not seen a sky that is completely dark. There is still a natural light up there, but one day there won't even be any light up there, and we will know. Our hearts will pound with excitement, "He is here at last!" We have waited for so long.

That is my message about the second coming, but my big question is: *why* is he coming back? That is the question that people don't ask, though I wish they would. I think they are just looking forward to seeing him face-to-face, but *why* should he come back to earth? What didn't he do the first time that he has got to come back to do? Above all, why is he emptying heaven when he comes back? Because he is bringing all of the people who have died in Christ with him—it says that. So all the saints who have died, including my daughter, my sister, her husband, my mother-in-law, all with Christ now, he is bringing back here. Why? If I am gone before he comes back, he will bring me back. Why, Lord? I want to stay in heaven. Why are you bringing me back to earth? Here, I have to tell you sadly, there is a huge division among Christians in the world as to *why* he is coming back. The Apostles' Creed, which I'm following, has got it wrong. It says that he is coming back here to judge the living and the dead. I believe that he will judge the living and the dead but he will not do that until *after* earth and sky have gone (Revelation 20:11).

Why then is he coming back to this earth and bringing all the saints in heaven with him? That is a huge logistic thing to do. Why does he need them all back here? This is a big division between professing Christians around the world. One group says he is coming back to judge, which doesn't fit the scripture. The other group says that he is coming back to reign, to rule — to take over the world until the nations of the world become the people of our God and his Messiah. That is what I firmly believe. If you ask another question, 'How long will he stay here on the second visit?' some Christians seem to think it will only be two minutes and then we will all be off again. So, why empty heaven, bring them all here, and then take them straight back up again? It would seem a bit of a waste of time and energy. No, I believe he is coming back to rule, to reign. For the first time, this world will have a Christian government.

He needs those saints to help him to take the world over. He will take the throne of the world and his saints will reign with him; Israel will reign with him because by that time they will be saved too. So saints will take over the world. There is part of me that dreads that because we can't even run the church properly now, and we are going to run the world! We must get into practice — we are going to rule the nations, Paul said it: we must be ready to judge each other because we are going to judge the nations. Our future destiny is to be the Christian government of the world. Jesus said, "When I get back I want to be able to say, 'Well done good and faithful servant, enter into the joy of your Lord. I'm going to put you in charge of ten cities.'" He meant that quite literally. We are going to take the world over: we will be governing the banks, we will be controlling the media. Can you imagine it? Not as we are — he had better do a lot more for us to get us ready for that, but it is all there in scripture.

Here is a hymn which was my favourite and I loved to sing when I was a boy. Perhaps because it had a very catchy tune, but something about it captured my little boy's heart even before I knew Christ.

> Sing we the King who is coming to reign,
> Sing we to Jesus the Lamb that was slain;
> Life and salvation His empire shall bring,
> Joy to the nations when Jesus is King.

All men shall dwell in His marvellous light,
Races long severed His love shall unite,
Justice and truth from His sceptre shall spring,
Wrong shall be ended when Jesus is King.

All shall be well in His Kingdom of peace,
Freedom shall flourish and wisdom increase,
Foe shall be friend when His triumph we sing,
Sword shall be sickle when Jesus is King.

Soul shall be saved from the burden of sin,
Doubt shall not darken His witness within,
Hell hath no terrors and Death hath no sting,
Love is victorious when Jesus is King.

Kingdom of Christ for your Coming we pray,
Hasten, O Father, the dawn of the day
When this new song Thy creation shall sing,
Satan is vanquished and Jesus is King.

Let me finish this chapter by showing you something. I
was in New York in between planes for about six hours, so
I got hold of a yellow taxi and said, "Take me around New
York, but particularly I want to go and visit the United
Nations not far from the Brooklyn Bridge." I had heard about
this magnificent building in which the UN meet, and I knew
it was open to visitors. So the taxi dropped me outside, and
there outside the main entrance was a block of granite stone
with half a verse of scripture on it. It is a bit dangerous to
only put half the verse as I'll show you, but there it was,
'And they shall beat their swords into ploughshares, and

their spears into pruning hooks: nation will not lift up sword against nation, neither shall they learn war anymore.' It is in Isaiah, but it is only half the verse. Then a young lady in blue uniform showed us around the United Nations—the general assembly room, the security room, the committee rooms. All the rooms were decorated with works of art from the whole world. It is a magnificent building. Then after two hours the little girl in blue uniform said, "Well, ladies and gentleman that completes our tour, have a nice day."

I said, "But you haven't shown us one room."

She said, "What room is that?" I told her. She said, "Oh that's closed, it's locked up. The public isn't allowed in that room."

"But I've come to the United Nations to see that room. I've been told about it, and I want to see it," I replied.

She said, "Well sorry, it's locked up. You can't see it."

"I've come all the way from little old England to see that room," I continued.

That really seems to appeal to American hearts somehow. She began to soften a bit. She said, "Well go down to the lobby, and get one of the guards, and ask him if he'll show you the room."

So I went down to the lobby and here was a man, about six foot ten I think, he looked it, with a couple of pistols in his belt.

I said, "The girl said to tell you that you should show me this room."

"No," he said, "that's closed to the public."

"But I've come all the way from little old England to see this room."

He said, "Well how long would you be in there?"

"Two minutes. I've just heard about it, I just want to see if what I've heard is true."

"Alright," and he took a key off a hook, and he took me across the lobby to a little door on one side of the lobby. He showed me into the room, and I saw the god of the United Nations, the god they pray to for world peace.

When that United Nations building was first built the first general secretary said, "We have no prayer room." So they built an extra room on between two of the wings. It has no windows but it is a wedge-shaped room squeezed in. They had a prayer room, and then the big debate began: what to put in it. Some wanted a cross; others didn't want a cross. The Hindus wanted flowers, the Muslims didn't want flowers. Finally, they approached a sculptor and said, "Would you fashion with your skilful hands something that would represent all the gods of the world that we can put in the prayer room?" He went away and he made a simple black block, painted in a matt black paint so you can't see any reflections from it—your eye goes right into it. He presented it to the United Nations and said, "Anybody can go in and kneel down to this and imagine their own god in there." So it represents all the gods of the world. It has no shape, so it can represent them all—then they put stools and prayer mats around it.

Now I had heard this and I thought, "Surely it's not true," but I've seen it. If you don't believe me, I could show you a photograph of it. That is the big black block that they pray to for peace in our world. I didn't know whether to laugh or cry, and I am not sure which I did. Praying to that for world peace? Actually the United Nations building is built in the wrong city. That text on the outside block of granite will never come true because of that. The first half of the verse says, 'When the Lord reigns in Zion, he will settle the disputes among the nations, and they will beat their swords into ploughshares, and their spears into pruning hooks.' You can't miss out that first half of the verse. I believe that one day the Lord will reign in Zion – in Jerusalem – and that is where the United Nations will be. Then there will be multilateral disarmament, and all the money we are spending on guns and bombs and mines will be spent to feed the hungry and clothe them. That is not a dream, God has promised it. It will happen. Praise be to his name!

7

The wonder of his
JUDGEMENT

In my private Bible study I use as many translations as I can get hold of, and I find some of the modern paraphrases very stimulating. In my morning devotions I have been reading a modern version of the Psalms. Here is one that is a very appropriate and refreshing version of Psalm 73:

No doubt about it! God is good — good to good people,
good to the good-hearted.
But I nearly missed it,
missed seeing his goodness.
I was looking the other way,
looking up to the people
At the top,
envying the wicked who have it made,
Who have nothing to worry about,
not a care in the whole wide world.

Pretentious with arrogance,
they wear the latest fashions in violence,
Pampered and overfed,
decked out in silk bows of silliness.
They jeer, using words to kill;
they bully their way with words.
They're full of hot air,

loudmouths disturbing the peace.
People actually listen to them—can you believe it?
Like thirsty puppies, they lap up their words.

What's going on here? Is God out to lunch?
Nobody's tending the store.
The wicked get by with everything;
they have it made, piling up riches.
I've been stupid to play by the rules;
what has it gotten me?
A long run of bad luck, that's what—
a slap in the face every time I walk out the door.

If I'd have given in and talked like this,
I would have betrayed your dear children.
Still, when I tried to figure it out,
all I got was a splitting headache . . .
Until I entered the sanctuary of God.
Then I saw the whole picture:
The slippery road you've put them on,
with a final crash in a ditch of delusions.
In the blink of an eye, disaster!
A blind curve in the dark, and—nightmare!
We wake up and rub our eyes....Nothing.
There's nothing to them. And there never was.

When I was beleaguered and bitter,
totally consumed by envy,
I was totally ignorant, a dumb ox
in your very presence.
I'm still in your presence,
but you've taken my hand.
You wisely and tenderly lead me,
and then you bless me.

You're all I want in heaven!
You're all I want on earth!
When my skin sags and my bones get brittle,
GOD is rock-firm and faithful.
Look! Those who left you are falling apart!
Deserters, they'll never be heard from again.
But I'm in the very presence of GOD —
oh, how refreshing it is!
I've made Lord GOD my home.
GOD, I'm telling the world what you do!

My last chapter about the wonders of Christ's story concerns the Day of Judgement. That is a very serious matter, but it is the last thing that Jesus will do for this world as it is. It is the second most frequent prediction in the New Testament.

The first most common prediction is that he is coming back. The second most common is that he will be the Judge of the whole world. Take one or two texts at random (I am breaking my own rule to tell you this): Acts 17:31, 'God has fixed a Day on which he will judge the world in righteousness by a Man whom he has appointed.' That was Paul preaching in Athens. Or take this: 'For we must all appear before the judgment seat of Christ, that each one may receive what is due to him for the things done while in the body, whether good or bad.' That was 2 Corinthians 5:10 (NIV). Here is one from Hebrews 9:27 (NIV), 'Just as man is destined to die once, and after that to face judgment....'

What we are saying is there are two appointments in God's diary for every one of us, and we don't know the date of either of them. The first appointment is the appointment with death. All of us will die unless the Lord comes back before — that is certain. Who was it that said there are only two certain things about life — death and taxes? He was a bit of a cynic, but it's true. It is appointed unto us to die and God knows that date and has it in his diary. But he has another appointment with us later, and that is the appointment for judgment. Every human being will keep those two appointments, which God has in his diary for every single human being. However, the first date will be different for all of us; the second date will be the same for all of us. The first date we face alone; the second date we face together, yet not as a crowd but as individuals. If there is one thing clear in the Bible, it is that we are judged as individuals, not as part of a family or as part of a church, but each person. We need to remember these two dates that we don't know, but which are fixed appointments. It is healthy to do so, it is not morbid.

We need to remember them, but we like to try to forget both if we can. We like to postpone the day of death; we like to forget that we are going to die. We attend the funerals of others, but we don't think about our own. We had a funeral director – an undertaker – in our town, and he had spent his life conducting funerals of others. He told me that he had never once thought that he was going to die. Isn't that amazing? Only when his little girl came to our Sunday school and went home and told him about Jesus, did he begin to think about his own death, and he came to Christ. I remember him giving his testimony. He said that he is socially unacceptable, and when he tells people, "I embalm bodies," and holds out his hand to shake theirs, they don't like doing so.

Nevertheless, we need to think about that second appointment—the Day of Judgement. Human beings instinctively want God to judge. It is an amazing contradiction: they don't want to be judged, but they do want God to judge. They tell him how he should be judging. They tell him, 'You should be judging us immediately; you should be judging us by our standards; and you should be judging everyone but me.' These are the three conditions of judgment that the world seems to want. First, they want him to be judging now, punishing the wicked now, dealing with the bad people now. I am always amused by the question, 'Why doesn't God get rid of all the bad people in the world and leave the rest of us to enjoy life happily, freely, and safely?' There is a flaw in that argument. It is the assumption that if God got rid of all the bad people, they would still be left. What a gigantic assumption, and it is a wrong assumption! Thank God, he is not going to judge the world immediately. Thank God, he's got patience. Thank God, he puts up with our badness, our rebellion, and our disobedience. But he has fixed a Day when accounts will be settled, when everything wrong will be put right, but he is very patient, and thank God he is.

I read somewhere that in America, sixty-six percent of the population are sure they are going to heaven and the same number is absolutely sure that they know someone who is going to hell. That is an interesting problem: the figures just don't add up. It is always others we want God to judge—we are alright, but if only God would get on with judging others. You know, we judge others by our standards. That is why, by our standards, other people deserve God's judgment and we don't, but then he doesn't judge by our standards.

God is strong on justice, but he is prepared to delay justice and hold it back for a good reason. It is a very simple reason: to give us time to repent. Otherwise he could step in tomorrow and judge the world and get rid of everybody who is spoiling the world for him, for each other, and even for themselves, but nobody would be left—nobody! We have all contributed to the world's problems. So if God got rid of everybody who is making the world worse, he would have to get rid of all of us, and that is the truth. But he is a Judge. He is a God of justice and mercy; he has shown us mercy now, but he will show justice later. Thank God he is doing it in that order because if he showed us justice now, there would be nobody left to show mercy to.

So, he is not going to judge immediately, but he is going to judge the world ultimately, not in this life but after we die. The whole world will be involved. That means that everybody will be called back to life. The Bible teaches the resurrection of the body for the righteous and the wicked. Daniel said that, Jesus said it, Paul says it. Everybody will be brought back to life. Indeed, it also says that all those drowned at sea will come back to life to be judged. Everybody who went down with the Titanic will be there. There must be thousands of people drowned in the sea and whose bodies have disintegrated in the water and gone. They did not find a single skeleton in the wreck of the Titanic; all the people had disintegrated and disappeared. They found some boots left, but no feet in them. But those people will be there. They will be raised from the depths of the ocean and find themselves standing before God.

So God delays to give us a full chance to repent, to put things right, and to choose good and not evil. That is why you cannot relate suffering in this world now directly to sin. There is general suffering in the world, but sometimes it is some of the greatest saints. Some of my best Christian friends have died of cancer. There is no direct correlation between sin and suffering in this world. That, of course, causes unrest and dissatisfaction because we live in an unjust world. The sooner we face that fact, the better we shall be able to live with it. It is an unjust world. It is an evil world by God's standards. Judgements don't seem directly related to how people live; that is why I quoted that Psalm. The psalmist said, 'I nearly slipped out of faith when I saw how wicked people survive and how the innocent suffer, and how bad people seem to get to the top of the social tree.' He said, 'I nearly slipped until I considered their end, where they were really heading.' He said, 'They're on a slippery slope to nothing; they really are worse off.' It takes faith to say that, to keep your faith though the innocent suffer sometimes and the bad people don't suffer.

Very simply, a Day is coming when God will put it right. No one gets away with anything in this world, though two-thirds of the crimes in my country are never discovered by the police, and therefore never brought to a court of law and never punished. Crime now pays in Britain. Only a minority of criminals are punished. We have young men who are breaking into the houses of elderly pensioners, retired people, and raping grandmothers of ninety and they are getting away with it.

Nobody will get away with anything before God. There will come a Day when all those crimes are back on the books, when people will face their own life. We had a very popular television show called *This is Your Life*. This took a person through their life and introduced people from their past. It was fascinating. The only problem with it was that they only showed us the good things. I talked to the researchers and they uncovered so many bad things which they had to suppress and leave out. So, the viewers were presented with such lovely, good people. One of them I knew and he was dismissed because he was dishonest; he was a rogue. He appeared on national television, *This is Your Life,* because of his exploits during World War Two. He was painted as a hero and we, who were watching, knew what he was really like. It was a very strange experience. I thought, 'What about all the others? All the great heroes we are presented with, I wonder what they discovered about them in secret?' The researchers had a file which was 'For your eyes only' and was kept firmly shut. But, on that Day, your whole life will be out.

God will present you with a book, *This is Your Life*, and even things you have forgotten, or suppressed into your subconscious, will all be there. It will be every word we have said and every thought we have thought and every feeling we have felt—but mainly, everything we have done. That is the word that is picked up every time judgment is mentioned in the New Testament. You are not judged by faith, what you believe; you are justified by faith. That is how you begin the Christian life, but everybody is judged by works, by what they have done in the body — what we have done in this life, between birth and death, and that will be the focus of the judgment. We should be judged by God's standards, not ours and not anybody else's.

What God expected of us will be the way we will be judged. As soon as people hear that, they come at me with this question: 'What about those who've never heard?' I have always replied to their question with another question and asked, 'So you're going to be a missionary?' They say, 'No.' But I say, 'I thought you were concerned about those who have never heard?' They are not really concerned about those who have never heard, they are trying to find a fault with God. Otherwise, they would join the missionary movement and go and tell people who have never heard. They are only trying to argue. But what do we believe? Those who have heard the gospel of Christ and his teaching will be judged by that. Those who have not heard, but have heard the Ten Commandments (we will say, some Jews who have not heard the Gospel but heard the Ten Commandments) will be judged by that. It is in Romans chapter 2 that Paul clearly teaches you will be judged not by what you didn't know, but by what you did.

It is furthermore the teaching of scripture that God has written some of his laws in the human heart, in the consciousness of everybody on earth. That is why every human being has some kind of standard between right and wrong. They have a law written within themselves that there is such a thing as right and wrong. It is very interesting: if we are only judged by the way we judge others that would be enough, because by our own sense of right and wrong we recognise wrong in other people so quickly. We are so slow to recognise it in ourselves. How often we condemn others by our standards, but we should be judged by those same standards. Which is why Jesus said, "Don't judge that you be not judged," because every time I say that somebody is doing something wrong, I am setting up a standard by which God will judge me. Hypocrisy is to judge others and not judge yourself by the same law of right and wrong. It does seem that everybody has something of the law of God written inside them.

To take one example: everybody in the world knows that abuse of children is wrong. Incest is condemned in every society on earth—isn't that interesting? Jesus taught that. He said, "Angels watch over children and it's better for you to have a millstone hung around your neck and thrown into the ocean than offend one of these little ones." God is very concerned about what we do to our children. Yet, on the internet, there are paedophiles abusing children the world over by the thousands. What does God think about that? Because everybody knows that is wrong, and the people who do it only do it because they think that nobody knows. That is the peril of the internet which you can watch privately. You think nobody is watching you and you can watch it all, privately. But God is watching and noting, and it is going down in the record. You see, those who don't fear God, those who don't think he exists, will do things secretly that they know are wrong, but they do them because they can get away with it and think that nobody knows. Nowadays, of course, they can actually find out if you are using your computer for something else and periodically the police break a paedophile ring. But, deep down, everybody knows that it is wrong to treat children like sex objects. God has written that into our hearts.

So, make no mistake, God is just. He is not unfair. He will judge everybody by what they knew and what they condemned in others as wrong. That is fair. He will not say, 'I reject you because you didn't respond to the gospel,' if they have never heard the gospel. That would be grossly unjust, but we can be assured that he judges by what we knew, what we have been told, what we were aware of in the right and wrong area. He is going to judge everybody — everybody who has ever lived. That is why the Bible teaches the resurrection of everybody, not just the saints. Everybody is going to have a new, immortal body and where they live with that body is going to be the result of his judgment.

The Bible not only talks about the laws of God, it talks about the *wrath* of God. That is a very important concept in the New Testament. I want to tell you something about the anger of God. There are two phases of God's anger. One is when it is simmering and the other is when it has boiled over. There are two different words in the New Testament for when God is feeling angry and when he is being angry. At the moment, God's anger is not boiling over; it will boil over on the Day of Judgement, but at the moment it is simmering like a pan of milk on the stove. You want to heat it up and then you take your eyes off it, and suddenly it is not just bubbling, it is all over the stove and you didn't expect it at that moment. Now you have to clean up the mess, and cleaning a burnt oven is not fun. I can tell you — I've watched my wife do it! But it was something that happened when she wasn't watching and didn't expect it, and it suddenly boiled over and messed up the meal.

There is evidence that God's wrath is simmering now. If you read Romans 1, you will find a description of what you can expect to see when God's anger is simmering over a society. In Romans chapter 1 it says, 'When people give God up, God gives people up' — which is only fair. When people give God up and he gives them up, the restraints are off, and human nature doesn't become better when God removes the restraints, but worse. One of the examples of becoming worse is a great increase in homosexuality. Now let me say this, which may shock you: I believe there is homosexuality in all of us, and that all of us are capable of it. When the restraints are off, any of us could get caught up in it. People go through phases, usually in the teens, when they are more attracted to their own sex than others. They get a crush on a teacher of the same sex. It is there. It is part of our fallen nature to want sex otherwise than God intended it to be used. We are all capable, it is just that in most of us it is restrained by many influences—by social opinion, by all kinds of things. But, when the brakes are off, we are all capable of anything.

I remember when Richard Wurmbrand came to our home. He was the Jewish pastor in Romania, who was in prison for so long. We had a very serious talk. He looked me in the face and said, "David, I could be a murderer." I looked at him. He is a lovely man. One of the loveliest things about him was that our three little children just fell in love with him — immediately they saw him they were climbing on his knee. When he said, "David, I could be a murderer," I said, "Richard, how do you know that?" He said, "I was in prison in Romania in a cell for two, and the other man was a Christian. Every day they tortured him and tried to make him deny Christ. Then they would throw him back in the cell, broken, bleeding, and he would collapse onto his bunk. Day after day they tortured him to make him deny Christ." He said, "One day he was thrown back in the cell and he was so weak he said, 'Richard, I can't take anymore. I've had so much pain; I cannot take another bit.' He said, 'Tomorrow, I shall deny Christ, I know.' He said, 'I just can't take it.'"

Richard lay awake that night and thought, 'He's going to deny Christ tomorrow.' Then the thought occurred to Richard, 'If I crept over while he's asleep and strangled him, he'll go to heaven without denying Christ.' He went over to his friend in the bunk and put his hands around his throat. The man opened his eyes and said, "Richard, what are you doing?" Richard said, "I was going to kill you to get you to heaven before you denied Christ." The man never did deny Christ from then on. He was tortured again and again until he died, but he never denied Christ. But, Richard was left with the knowledge that he could be a murderer. Given sufficient pressure, he knew he would kill a human being. He said that brought him to a realisation that in our fallen nature are all the sins—but our upbringing, our society, so many things restrain us.

Above all, God puts the brakes on our fallen nature. It is when God withdraws his Spirit from us, and from our society, that violence and perverted sex comes sweeping in. So God's anger is simmering over the Western world. It has not boiled over yet. The Bible says one day there will be a Day of God's wrath, when it boils over. Those who see it simmering now, who see the symptoms in society, see the breakup of family life, see social irresponsibility; read Romans 1 and it gives you all the symptoms of society with which God is already angry, but it is simmering. One day, the Day of wrath, it boils over and God deals with everything justly. We live in an unjust world, an unjust society, but one day God's justice will deal with the whole thing. Wrong will be put right, judged and dealt with. That is the Day of Judgement.

Now, let us go a little further. It comes as a surprise to

many if you say that God will not judge the human race. When the great white throne appears and the world appears before it, it will not be God on that throne. Who will judge the world? God has deliberately delegated the judgment of the world to a Man called Jesus. Jesus the Saviour will be the Judge. Many people only look at Jesus' first coming as Saviour and think they know Jesus, but the Bible talks about his second coming as Judge. That is the same Jesus, but with a very different mission. He came first to save us, but he will come second to judge us. That is the whole truth about Jesus.

This is why many Christians ignore the book of Revelation, because it talks about Jesus judging the world, not saving it. It says in the book of Revelation that the world will shrink from him in fear and cry for the mountains to come and fall on them to hide them from the face of Jesus. What an extraordinary situation! It is the same Jesus, but now he is showing a very different side to his character, a side that was always there. It was there when in anger he cleansed the temple; it was there when he healed a man with a withered hand and was criticised for it and he was angry with those who criticised him for healing on the Sabbath. There were glimpses of this Jesus even the first time, but only glimpses. When he comes the second time, it will all be laid bare. People are going to get a shock, that the one whom they thought in Sunday school was 'gentle Jesus, meek and mild' is dealing with his enemies. So, who will be the Judge, if not God? Christian creeds make it quite clear that Jesus will be the judge... and what a difference that makes. It means that he has the right to judge —because he has been in our world; he has been under our pressures; he has been tempted at all points. If anyone has the right to judge the human race it is

Jesus, and the world will be silent before him.

Not only that, but Jesus knows everything about us. That surprised the woman at the well at Samaria: "You've had five husbands and the man you're living with is not your husband at all." She was shaken that he knew all about her. Jesus knows all about me; he knows all about you. In fact, I am going to tell you something about me: I have written my life's story. I have called it *Not as Bad as the Truth,* which may sound like a funny title for your autobiography. But years ago, there were people in a place called Wales, who spread rumours about me which were totally untrue; they were lies. They began to spread all over England as if people loved to believe the worst. I began to get letters saying, 'Dear Mr Pawson, we are very sorry, but arrangements for your visit have fallen through.' They never told me why, but I knew they had heard the rumours. It was painful for my wife. She knew they were not true and I went and complained to the Lord bitterly.

I said, "Lord, it's not only painful that they're telling lies, but it's spoiling my ministry. It's closing doors to me."

Do you know what the Lord said? He said, "David, the worst they could say about you is not as bad as the truth."

Do you know what? I burst out laughing with relief that my critics didn't know the truth. Then he added, "I know the worst and I still love you and use you."

That somehow cleared it up. I went through to the kitchen and I said, "Do you know what the Lord just said to me? He just said, 'The worst people say about you is not as bad as the truth.'" My wife just about fell on the floor laughing — that was it. On that day, I made up my mind if ever I told my life story it would be called *Not as Bad as the Truth*. I realised then that the Lord knows everything about me. Did you ever realise that he not only knows it all, but he has written it all down in his books?

One day the books will be opened and they will not just be opened to you but open to the public, because God's justice must be seen to be done; it must be public. The Day of Judgement we face as individuals, but it is a very public occasion, when all your life will be opened to view. That is enough to bring us to a sober position. Books will be opened, everything we have done will be revealed; even, said Jesus, secrets in the bedroom will be shouted from the house tops. That is the Day of Judgement.

Who then, will be acquitted? Who will be judged innocent in that Day? Well, quite frankly, nobody. I haven't met anybody who would be happy to have their whole life laid bare for the public to know. All of us have secrets. All of us have some regrets and we would not like them to come out. Yet on that Day there will be two groups—one acquitted, and the other guilty. To one, Jesus, himself will say, "Come, you blessed of my Father, inherit the Kingdom." To the others he will say, "Depart from me, you cursed, into the place prepared for the devil and his angels." Do you realise that hell was never prepared for human beings? It was prepared for the devil and all his angels, because Jesus did not die for a single angel. We know from the scripture that a third of the angels have rebelled in heaven, led by Satan, who is an angel. We call the angels who followed him 'demons', but that is what they were and that is what they are—fallen angels. There is no salvation, no forgiveness available for angels. Therefore God had to prepare a place where he could put them because angels do have immortality. Hell was prepared for them, not for any of us. However, if we are not acquitted on that Day, we are sentenced to live with the devil and all his angels forever and ever afterwards.

I can think of nothing worse than knowing that there is no hope of getting out of there. That is why Jesus kept using quite a severe phrase—"weeping and gnashing of teeth". That tells me it is a mixture of regret and frustration: gnashing of teeth, knowing you cannot get out of there, knowing you are there forever. That is why I wrote the book on hell: *The Road to Hell*. Unfortunately, more and more preachers today don't believe in hell. They don't preach it; they don't teach it. They talk about the 'unconditional love of God', which of course could never throw anybody into hell. But, Jesus said more about hell than any other person in the Bible. In fact, nobody else talks about hell in the whole Bible. Everything I know about hell, I have learned from Jesus. From his lips we were given the truth and the whole truth.

Oh, but listen: it says books were opened on that Day, books of our lives, the record of what we have done in the body, meaning in this world. But, there is another book that is also open. It is not our book, it is called 'The Lamb's Book of Life'. It is his book and in it there are hundreds and hundreds of names, and yet, it is his book, the only one who lived on this earth and never gave way to Satan. Jesus was tempted in every point just as we are, yet never sinned. It is Jesus' book and it is the only book acceptable to God. But, there are hundreds of names in that book and I trust your name is in it because on that Day, when that book is opened, the other books are shut. If your name is in the Lamb's Book of Life, that Day will not be a threat to you.

So how do you get your name into the Lamb's Book of Life? The answer is by having your sins forgiven, and then, because Jesus died for you and paid for your sin already, you can be acquitted, justified in God's sight, put in his good book.

However, there is something more to say. I told you how you get your name into the Book of Life, the Lamb's Book of Life—but you know, the Book of Life is only mentioned four times in the whole Bible and three of those times talk about names being blotted out of his book.

So, my second point I want to make very strongly. I have told you how you *get* your name in the book, but how do you *keep* it in, given that three out of four references to the Lamb's Book of Life talk about names being blotted out of that book? It can be ripped out. God has made a promise, through Jesus, to us in the book of Revelation again, chapter three: "Blessed is he who overcomes. His name will not be blotted out of the Book of Life." If language means anything, it means that believers who don't overcome will have their names removed. That is serious. You know your name is in that book when you've had your sins forgiven, but *keep* it in. There is something else needed to keep it in. Forgiveness gets your name into the book, but *holiness* keeps it in. You need holiness as well as forgiveness. Those are the two greatest needs for every human heart to be ready for God's new world. It says at the end of Revelation that not all believers will inherit the new heavens and the new earth, but those who overcome will inherit all this.

What does 'overcome' mean? It means those who have overcome pressures from outside and inside, from persecution outside and from temptation inside. It is overcomers who will inherit the new heaven and the new earth. Read chapter twenty-one of Revelation. It is those who give in and those who don't come out on top, but go under—it is they whose names are taken out of the Book of Life. Oh, I pray that when that great Day comes, my name will still be in there and yours will still be in there. God knows that not only have we been forgiven, but we are pressing on to that holiness without which no man will see the Lord.

That is my serious word. Judgement is a serious subject and I am finishing on that serious note. The good news is that God doesn't say to us, "I'll give you forgiveness and you produce holiness." That's to *offer* forgiveness and *demand* holiness. But, in my Bible, God offers forgiveness and holiness; they are both gifts, but they both need to be received and appropriated. They are both there for you. You get your name in when you receive his forgiveness; you keep it in when you're willing to receive his holiness. Both are an offer; both are freely offered in the gospel of Jesus Christ; both are needed. So, when the Day comes, may your name and mine be in the right book. I don't want the name on my book; I don't want it to be read. I want my name to be in *his* book and stay there for all eternity.

Let us finish with this quote from Revelation: 'If anyone's name was not found written in the Book of Life, he was thrown into the lake of fire.' God grant that may never be said of us. Amen.

Epilogue

YOUR STORY?

A German pastor once told me his unusual story. As a boy he had volunteered for the Hitler Youth Movement and was interviewed by an officer. The interrogation went as follows:

"Where do you live, boy?"

"In Hamburg, sir."

"I said, where do you live?"

"In Germany, sir?"

"The wrong answer, where do you live?"

"In the Third Reich, sir." [*reich* = kingdom]

"Still wrong."

"I don't know what you want me to say, sir."

"From now on you must say: I live in Hitler."

From that moment he lived in, by, with and for his Fuehrer (= master). He fought in World War II in the Wehrmacht (army), was taken prisoner by the British and was confined in a prisoner of war camp in East Anglia. A local resident came and talked to him through the barbed wire fence and even shared part of his meagre food ration with the hungry internee far from home. Later, when prisoners were allowed out to work on local farms, this one made a point of finding out who his new friend and benefactor was. It turned out to be a Methodist lay preacher, who shared the gospel with him, leading him to repentance and faith. Now he shepherds the flock of a church in his *heimat* (homeland). As he told me: "I used to live in Hitler," then his face lit up and he added: "but now I live in Christ."

The shortest and simplest definition of a 'Christian' is that it is someone who is 'in Christ' (by crossing out the 'a' and reversing the two words that are left). Evangelists are perhaps a little too prone to urge their hearers to 'invite Jesus into' their lives, to 'come and live in' their hearts. But this can leave an impression that Jesus is smaller than we are, whereas he is much greater. It is true that Paul once (only) said: 'Christ in us'; but far more frequently he put it the other way round and wrote about himself and his readers being 'in Christ'. So it would be more meaningful to urge people to come into *his* life than to ask him to come into theirs.

I have only told you half the story until now: how he identified himself with us, experiencing for himself our humanity in his life and our inhumanity in his death. But you, dear reader, need to complete the story by identifying yourself with him. Knowing more *about* him than you did is one thing, but knowing *him* better is another. I mean knowing him personally, to talk to. You could put this book down right now and just do exactly that. Realising all that he has done, is doing and will do to save you from yourself and this sad and sinful world should give you plenty to talk about, even just a very big 'thank-you' and a very deep 'sorry' for not realising it sooner.

Above all, ask him to exchange your life with his. To quote the apostle Paul: 'God made him who had no sin to be sin for us, so that in him we might become the righteousness of God' (2 Corinthians 5:21, NIV). What a bargain! Our sin for his righteousness, our life for his.

Amazingly, all that you have read about becomes your story as well as his! The seven wonders are applied in scripture to all who 'follow' Jesus all the way.

They have been born of the Holy Spirit.
(John 3:5; Titus 3:5)

They have been crucified with Christ.
(Galatians 5:24; Colossians 3:3)

They have been buried with him.
(Romans 6:4; Colossians 2:11–12)

They have been raised with him.
(Colossians 3:1)

They have ascended with him.
(Ephesians 2:6).

They will return with him.
(1 Thessalonians 4:14)

They will judge with him.
(1 Corinthians 6:2)

Try reading this last list substituting "I" for 'they'. Does that feel comfortable, reassuring? Does his story fit you? It was meant to. It was intended all along, by the heavenly Father himself. In fact he only made us because he so loved and enjoyed his only son that he wanted a bigger family, provided we turned out just like him. (Romans 8:29) So when his life becomes ours, God will be as pleased with us as he was with him (Matthew 3:17). Have you noticed that I've started putting in scripture references (books, chapter and verse numbers)? I could have done this all through the book but didn't want to interrupt the flow of the story. Now I want you to know where I got it all from. Without my Bible I would still be totally ignorant of the 'seven wonders'. It is by meditating on its pages, using my reason, emotions and imagination and any relevant information I can pick up elsewhere, that I have been able to tell you 'the greatest story ever told'.

To help you make the same thrilling discoveries, I wrote another, much bigger, book, called 'Unlocking the Bible', in which I open up all sixty-six books of the Bible as they have been opened up to me. In fact, every one of them adds something to the picture of Jesus as he really is. When he said the 'scriptures' all point to him, he was referring to the *Old* Testament; none of the New had yet been written (John 5:39). So if you have found this book enlightening, that one would be an ideal follow-up. Thousands have found it as exciting to read as I found putting it all together.

And may your story, like his, have a happy ending (Hebrews 12:2). Except that his will never end. Neither need yours. You can live 'happily ever after' in him.

EBOOKS

Most books by David Pawson are also available
as ebooks from:

amazon.com and amazon.co.uk Kindle stores.

**For details of foreign language editions
and a full listing of
David Pawson Teaching Catalogue in MP3/DVD
or to purchase David Pawson books in the** UK
please visit:
www.davidpawson.com

Email: info@davidpawsonministry.com

Chinese language books by David Pawson
www.bolbookstore.com
and
www.elimbookstore.com.tw